# THE SKY OF THE HEART

# THE SKY OF THE HEART

*Jewels of Wisdom from Nityananda*

Introduction and commentary
by Swami Chetanananda

Originally translated by M.U. Hatengdi

RUDRA PRESS  *Portland, Oregon*

Rudra Press
PO Box 13390
Portland, Oregon 97213
Telephone: (503) 235-0175
Telefax: (503) 235-0909

Book and cover design: Bill Stanton
Illustrations: Ana Capitaine
Photographs: M.D. Suvarna
Sutras editor: Cheryl Berling Rosen

Nityananda, Swami, 1897–1961
The sky of the heart : jewels of wisdom from Nityananda / compiled
and translated by M.U. Hatengdi and Swami Chetanananda ; with
preface, introduction, and commentary.
    p. cm.
  ISBN 0-915801-63-9 (alk. paper)
    I. Spiritual life—Hinduism.   I. Hatengdi, M.U., 1914–
II. Chetanananda, Swami, 1948–   . III. Title.
BL1237.32.N57  1996
294.5'4—dc20
                                            96-7523
                                              CIP

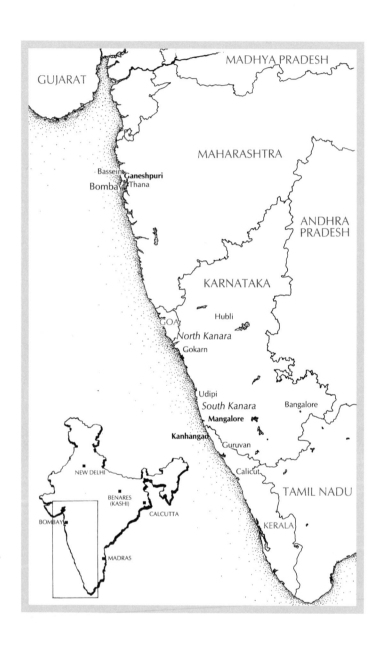

GUJARAT

MADHYA PRADESH

MAHARASHTRA

Bassein — **Ganeshpuri**
Bombay — Thana

ANDHRA
PRADESH

KARNATAKA

Hubli

GOA

*North Kanara*

Gokarn

Udipi
*South Kanara*

Bangalore

**Mangalore**

**Kanhangad**

Guruvan

Calicut

TAMIL NADU

NEW DELHI

BENARES
(KASHI)

CALCUTTA

BOMBAY

KERALA

MADRAS

# Contents

Preface by M.U. Hatengdi    ix

Introduction by Swami Chetanananda    1

The Self    35

The Higher Mind    95

The Power of Om    133

Spiritual Practice    159

Commentary    247

Glossary    267

About M.U. Hatengdi    287

About Swami Chetanananda    289

# Preface

Rivers in the east flow eastward, rivers in the west flow westward, and they all enter the sea. From sea to sea they pass, the clouds lifting them to the sky as vapor and sending them down as rain. And as these rivers, when they are united with the sea, do not know whether they are this river or that, likewise all creatures when they return from Brahman (God Infinite) do not know from whence they came.

—from the Chandogya Upanishad

IN AN ATTEMPT TO PROJECT in English an image of the immortal Master of Ganeshpuri, I collected a number of authenticated stories illustrative of the life of Nityananda covering a period of nearly four decades. Thanks to the interest evinced by Swami

Chetanananda of the United States and the editorial efforts of members of the Nityananda Institute, these were presented to the Western reader in *Nityananda: The Divine Presence* (Rudra Press, 1984).

Although that book contained words spoken by Nityananda at Ganeshpuri and published for the first time, I was aware of the inherent inadequacy of words in defining a divine personality. Such comprehension generally is held to come only to minds imbued with purity of motive and with a keen inclination toward attaining yoga. Hence Nityananda exhorted devotees and even first visitors to cultivate *shuddha bhavana* (purity of motive) and *shraddha* (keen inclination toward yoga). As Krishna says in the Bhagavad Gita:

> Fools pass blindly by the place of my dwelling
> Here in the human form, and of my majesty
> They know nothing at all,
> Who am the Lord, their soul. [9:11]

In Nityananda's case, the situation was further confused by his silence toward the general public and the resulting anonymity surrounding his physical manifestation, movements, and activities.

In this edition we attempt a fresh English rendering of these words, originally called the *Chidakash Gita* and attributed to him in his youthful days in Mangalore sometime between 1922 and 1924. At this time he would start a monologue in whichever devotee's house he happened to find himself at that particular moment. After some time he would stop. Listening devotees initially mistook what he said for gibberish. Later, however, they discovered two special points connected with these monologues. First, the words so uttered contained pearls of wisdom. Considering that Nityananda was illiterate in the academic sense, they inferred that he could have only uttered them from an exalted state of personal experience. Second, these monologues were preceded invariably by a hailing of Arjuna, asking him to come and listen to Krishna. Arjuna is the hero of the Mahabharata and the one to whom the dialogue known as the Bhagavad Gita is revealed by Krishna. Nityananda's actual words were "Arjuna-mama, come and listen. Krishna-ajja is going to speak." (The suffix "mama" literally means maternal uncle; "ajja" means grandfather.)

As a result, devotees started keeping paper and pencils handy to take notes as soon as Arjuna was hailed. As the location of these monologues changed, so did the devotee recorders who, by no means, were highly literate themselves. Nonetheless, they were all devout, sincere, and had the highest respect for the youthful Nityananda. This devotion aided them in recording his words because he was not always coherent, speaking as if from a trance-like condition. After some time, these monologue sessions ended and

Tulsiamma, a senior woman devotee, collected and collated the notes taken down by the several devotees. They then turned to Nityananda for instructions about their publication. He told them that the words had come from *chidakash* (the ether of awareness or a state of cosmic consciousness) and were not intended to be written down. Whether they were ever published or read, "this one" (as he would have said since Nityananda never referred to himself in the first person) was disinterested.

However, Tulsiamma got the notes published in the south Indian language of Kanarese as *Chidakash Gita* (Song from the Sky of Consciousness). Strictly speaking, the words spoken are more appropriately called *srutis*, or divinely revealed wisdom, rather that *gita*, which means song or poem. Subsequently, several Kanarese and two English translations appeared, the latter two in 1940 and around 1963. I undertook a fresh English rendering of these selected sutras in an attempt to make the deeper meanings underlying these laconic expressions available to the layperson as well as to supplement *Nityananda: The Divine Presence* in portraying his image. The stories therein are like so many floral tributes providing through their hue and fragrance a mosaic image, as it were, of a great mystic personality. In this volume, his words present a clearer image because they come not from books but from his own experience while in a state of cosmic consciousness.

While the sutras describe the qualities of an ideal Guru, I would like to add those of an ideal devotee as described by a certain South Indian saint. First, he says, ideal devotees are born like Faith incarnate with an intense longing for the ultimate union of the individual with the Universal. Second, oblivious of any special talents or attainments he or she might possess, such devotees always sing the glories of the Master. Third, such a devotee is like a flute played and guided by the hands of the Master. Next, an ideal devotee is like the hospitable cowherd who milks the cows and distributes the bounty to the needy: The Guru is the cow, the milk is knowledge, the needy are the devotees hungering for it. Finally, the saint says that such devotees are superior to camphor. This analogy refers to the purity of the camphor waved in ceremonies (*ariti*) throughout India before deities in temples and shrines. But whereas camphor burns itself out lighting up the deity for a time, ideal devotees by their tributes immortalize the Master for all time.

Nityananda was a silent saint and not an organization man. His thoughts live through eternity to enter human hearts and minds throughout the world, raising up men and women to achieve varying degrees of success in the practical expression of the workings of their lives. He was the type of saint that helps and inspires multitudes of householders, worldly people, or renunciates to the greatest extent, without any overt aids and regardless of a person's close physical proximity to him. In this way he consoled a grieving devotee with an intuitive premonition of the saint's passing away three months before the actual event, knowing that more could be achieved in the subtle than in the gross. In truth, few of the hundreds of devotees that now daily throng to his samadhi shrine ever saw him in his physical form. And yet when you enquire of them as to why they come, each one has a tale to tell in which some distress was relieved, guidance received, or elevation of spirit experienced.

The editors of the Nityananda Institute and Rudra Press have helped make this volume what it is today. Through their perseverance and genuine love for the manuscript, they have pruned the elaborate commentaries that I initially provided so that the pregnant words of Nityananda shine on their own, unclouded by semantics and extraneous references. I am grateful to them and to Swami Chetanananda for publishing these books in the United States.

If *The Sky of the Heart* and its companion volume achieve even to a limited extent the projection of Nityananda's occult image and help the Reader appreciate eternal values by attempting to live up to them in a fast-changing and troubled world, I would have more than achieved my aim in compiling and writing them.

"Sir," said a pupil to his master, "teach me the nature of Brahman (God infinite)." The master did not reply. When a second and third time he was importuned, he answered: "I teach you indeed, but you do not follow. His name is silence."

—from Shankara's commentary on the Kena Upanishad

*M.U. Hatengdi*

# Introduction

FOR CENTURIES WESTERNERS have seen India as a land of magic and mystery. Western writers describe both fiery-eyed mystics performing apparent feats of magic as well as a rigorous system of scholarship in philosophy pursued with energy and precision for thousands of years. India is a land of stunning and overwhelming contrasts. But of all its extraordinary and mysterious features, one of the most amazing is that every fifty years or so she is gifted with the presence of a great realized being—a *mahatma*. Such a person is born totally pure, innately free of any attachment whatsoever to the world and to worldly things. Because of the mahatma's total immersion in the Divine and Universal, the flow of energy through his or her being is remarkable. Nityananda was such a being—a mahatma of incredible, awesome yogic power and capacity.

The presence that was Nityananda had very little to do with his body and everything to do with the great spiritual force of which his body was merely a beacon. His body was simply a sign pointing to the deep and endless well of spiritual power. And such a well does not belong to any personality.

Americans do not think easily in these terms. Although we have seen many gurus in the past several decades, it is impossible for us to really fathom who or what Nityananda was because his state of being at no point corresponds to ordinary individual experience as Americans know it. Among the gurus who have been here, only a few were great beings, many were great showmen, and a few were charlatans. As a result, Americans question deeply both the nature of the guru and the need for one. We are unprepared for someone like Nityananda. Culturally, we have no precedents or criteria by which to classify a person whose very nature is detachment.

Nityananda had no purpose in the world and no message to bring. Why he appeared is unknown to anyone except perhaps himself. He was born to the austerity in which he lived his life. Simplicity and detachment were his essential nature—not something trained for or contemplated. His greatness was completely natural to him.

Yet detachment this complete is totally unfamiliar to us, even shocking. For example, people often brought him offerings of fruit, which, by week's end, might add up to tons of food. Often Nityananda just let it rot. It was not that he was stingy or did not want to give it away; in a way, he did not even notice that it was there. He was that disinterested in things external. All the fruit, flowers, and other gifts that appeared were like raindrops falling from the sky. It never occurred to him to do anything with objects that manifested around him.

Most of us think that in order to pursue a spiritual life, we need something different from what we already know; a different idea, philosophy, or life-style. Nityananda made no such demands. He did not promote a particular life-style, philosophy, or perspective. He was not a teacher of any method and he did nothing to establish an organization around him. He never gave the required programs, intensives, workshops, or seminars assumed by modern-day mentalities, and he never asked for money. People came to him and he blessed them, he uplifted them, he gave them whatever they were able to take from him. It was just that simple and that free.

He brought tremendous peace and betterment to the simple people; the poor and the destitute were especially drawn to his simplicity and lack of judgment. As time went on, he touched the lives of countless people of all classes, showering miracles of healing and upliftment upon many. He sought no one's approval, recognition, or promotion for this. He lived in the jungle where people had to seek him out. Nityananda was a very simple man who dedicated his life to the presence of the Divine and who lived each day as a beacon of that presence.

To approach Nityananda, we must suspend all judgment. His words are profound and the subject is nothing less than the essence of Life itself.

## Background

Nityananda lived from the late nineteenth century to 1961, making him one of India's most recent extraordinary saints. Nonetheless, information about his birth and early childhood is sparse and contradictory. In *Nityananda: The Divine Presence* (Rudra Press, 1984) it is said that as an infant he was found in the Guruvan jungle by a *harijan* woman. This woman sold the baby to the childless Unniamma of Calicut, a simple woman who earned a small income by doing household work for Ishwar Iyer, a prominent solicitor. This kind, devout man took an interest in the youngster, who was named Ram by his adoptive mother. Upon her death, he assumed guardianship of the child.

Occasional remarks made by Nityananda through the years, however, support another version: Protected by a large serpent coiled around him, the baby was found on a riverbank and cared for by the kind-hearted but poor Unniamma, here married with several children of her own. Ishwar Iyer, again Unniamma's employer, took in the orphaned Ram upon her death.

A few stories of his boyhood pranks survive and are recounted in *Nityananda: The Divine Presence*. It is generally agreed that Ram, as he was then called, left his home with Mr. Iyer following a trip the two took together to Benares. He was then perhaps in his early teens and it is known that he traveled widely during this period. While it is impossible to reconstruct an itinerary, it is thought that he spent considerable time in the Himalayas and in many holy places in north India. When his foster father lay dying, Nityananda returned to Calicut to be with him. Following the funeral, Nityananda again departed for a period of wandering in south India, and stories exist of even more far-ranging travel: to Singapore, Malaysia, even Japan.

Whether or not Nityananda had a guru has been a source of considerable discussion. It is my belief that everybody has a guru. Although Nityananda never talked about it, and although confusion arises about how it might have happened, I feel that undoubtedly someone was there to awaken within Nityananda his inner spiritual force. This force is like the great power and intense pressure of an oil well— it is always present but needs to be tapped. Once tapped, the immense and powerful richness explodes to the surface. In the same way, someone tapped the well in Nityananda. Whether it followed a long association or a momentary meeting, whether it was someone in the Himalayas or Singapore or Ishwar Iyer or even Shivananda, no one knows —and it is not important. What is important is that some contact took place to tap the well and allow the greatness therein to come to the surface where it continues to affect our lives today.

Around 1910 stories begin placing the young Nityananda in the South Kanara district of North Kerala. This was a time of miracles and of growing recognition that an exceptional being was present. Historically, Nityananda was discovered in Udipi in 1918 by two gentlemen who remained life-long devotees.

During this period Nityananda traveled a great deal. He also spent time in contemplation at Guruvan, the jungle where he was found as an infant. For a time he stayed a few miles nearer the sea at Kanhangad, starting several substantial building projects and working on the rock-cut caves for which the area is famous. By now he was quite well known and an ashram was developing around him. Today we find temples to his honor at both Guruvan and Kanhangad.

He spoke the words translated here during the early 1920s in Mangalore. Nityananda had many devotees here and it was his custom to stay with a devotee family in the town and allow others to sit with him in the evenings. Several photographs from these years are reproduced in this volume.

In the mid-1930s he settled in a jungle near Bombay called Ganeshpuri. There he remained for almost thirty years, until his *mahasamadhi* in 1961. His reputation grew steadily during this time, drawing crowds to this tiny place in the jungle. Initially, he stayed at a very old Shiva temple called the Bhimeshwari temple. Built in the sixth or seventh century, the site was overgrown by vegetation and inhabited by snakes and tigers. Nityananda cleared it out and settled into this simple temple, which was just a hollow place lined with stones and covered with a roof. In the center of the floor stood a round stone pillar called a *lingham*. Villagers would pour water over it and decorate it with flowers and *kumkum*, the vermilion powder used in worship and ceremonies. The lingham is the symbol of Shiva's pure potential. And because Nityananda was there, the sixty or seventy miles surrounding Ganeshpuri were transformed from a jungle to a place where the ground was cultivated and educated people came to live.

Nityananda was an *avadhut*. Many people considered him to be an incarnation of Ganesha, the son of Shiva and Parvati. Wearing only a loincloth, he lived as a total renunciate, a *sannyasi*. For years he only took food from someone else's hand, and the food was very simple: some fruit, a few vegetables, a little coffee. He spent his days in meditation. Even in his later life, while receiving thousands of people for *darshan*, his state remained the same.

From his presence, miracles of healing, of understanding, of the bestowal of peace and joy flowed. The credit for these things he gave to God and to the faith and devotion of the seeker. He would say, "Everything that happens, happens automatically by the will of God." Therefore, everything was possible. Miracles occurred naturally around him because of his continuous state of perfect Self-realization. He was always in union with the inner Self, and the need for this union was at the heart of his teaching. Like ancient sages from many traditions, he said that anyone who merges the individual into the universal is enlightened.

The goal of spiritual practice (*sadhana*) is to merge one's individual consciousness into divine consciousness; to merge creative energy (*Shakti*) into the seat of consciousness (*Shiva*). A person established thusly (in what Nityananda called the *chidakash*) puts an end to the wanderings and the multiplicities that manifest in the self. A person who lives in the Supreme Self lives beyond space and time and dwells in infinity, where all past lives are known and ended and where all past karmas are dissolved. Such a person lives the pure, beautiful, abundant experience of the Supreme Self.

## The Sutras

The sutras presented in *The Sky of the Heart* demonstrate Nityananda's mastery of spirituality, speaking as he does with simple conviction about the most subtle and refined points of the spiritual realm. And because he spoke very little, these sutras are a rare treasure of inspired wisdom arising from a special state of consciousness.

They date from the early 1920s in Mangalore when devotees gathered around Nityananda each evening to sit in silence. Occasionally, however, Nityananda would speak from a trance-like state, and eventually the devotees began to copy down his words. It must be remembered that the many transcribers spoke different dialects and had varying levels of education. Sometimes his words were not recorded until after Nityananda had stopped speaking for the evening. Years later, these notes in their various formats and languages were gathered together and compiled by a persevering devotee and published in the Kanarese dialect. Other translations and versions have since appeared in several languages and dialects, including three previous English versions.

The Reader should not study these sutras with an intellectual agenda of trying to understand every word. To do so would be to miss the spirit of our endeavor. We publish this volume in order to give people direct contact with

Nityananda's wisdom and to reveal something of what went on in his mind, what he did, and what his spiritual practices were. Nityananda first and foremost was concerned with immersing the mind in the inner Self. He had no interest in consistency or intellectual acuity. In fact, there is no record that Nityananda even received a formal education outside of Mr. Iyer's home. He was not an intellectual, he was not a scholar; in truth, he was not even a teacher in that his purpose was not to inspire anyone. Nityananda lived in and from the Self—and that was his existence.

He was not concerned about differences between systems and philosophies and his language was certainly not rigorously philosophical. Whether a term was Vedantic and from the Shankara school or whether it was Tantric or Buddhist did not interest him. Nityananda used terms from all of India's great traditions without distinction. His vision was universal and he used language that common people would understand. Occasionally and to no avail, visitors to Ganeshpuri would try to engage him in scholarly debate. "What are your thoughts on the Bhagavad Gita?" they would ask him. "From beginning to end, it is advice to renounce, renounce, renounce. What else is there?" he told one scholar. Even when using the words "Vedanta" or "Veda," he was not referring to a specific philosophical system or sacred text. He was simply referring to truth and knowledge: Veda as knowledge and Vedanta as the goal of the Vedas.

## The Philosophy

> The essential knowledge must be attained by everyone.
> And what is this essential knowledge? For the individual
> Self to know the mystery of the universal Self. (Sutra 51)

Both the mystery and wisdom of Nityananda's words arise from the same understanding: *everything is one.* To fulfill the requirement for liberation and merge the individual in the Divine, we must understand that there is no inherent difference between the two. The apparent difference, and thereby all the confusion and multiplicity of life, in fact, is simply a misunderstanding. It is *maya.* The life-force, the dynamic creative energy that is the source and sustenance of our individual lives, is the same creative energy that moves in all things and in all places. Thus, the study of yoga is the study of the Self, of our own life-force. The more we study it, the more we realize that there is nothing outside of it. The simple, fundamental ground of our own being permeates all that is. All experience manifests on the same field of pure consciousness, and this consciousness that moves in us moves in everyone and everything. The Self *is* the Absolute —to which we have intimate, personal access.

# The Nature of the Absolute

> This is Shiva-Shakti, the creative power of the indivisible One. And God's creative power is the Self, the One reality. (Sutra 63)

The Absolute, the ultimate reality, the highest of all—this is pure consciousness. This pure dynamic consciousness is the basis and source of all manifestation, large and small. Many names have been given to this "ground of all": Shiva, Parashakti, Parabrahma, Atman, the Self, God. It is the divine consciousness in all, the one consciousness. This ocean of pure potentiality has two inseparable aspects: pure potential (Shiva) and pure energy (Shakti). Shakti is the supreme creative aspect of the Absolute, vital and dynamic. It is both completely stable and never still, the eternally pulsating sound and power of om: the creative energy of Life, *omkar*.

Within the sea of pure consciousness, this resonance causes movement, waves, and ripples that intersect and mingle, rise and break. All manifestation arises from the movement and interaction of forces precipitated by the resonance that is Omkar. Omkar is the original word (*paravac*), the universal sound (*shabda*), the "Word" in the Gospel of St. John ("In the beginning was the Word and the Word was with God and the Word was God." John 6:1). In the Rig Veda, one of the most ancient of Indian holy texts, Omkar is *vac*, creator and substance of all. Omkar is pulsating everywhere, always at the same time. It is form-less, completely open, pure potential.

> Om vibrates like a storm in the sky. Having neither beginning nor end, it is the stage manager of the Divine Drama. The human body is a string of Om, all that is— inside us, outside us—is born of Om. (Sutra 95)

Omkar—Shakti—is the very nature of the Absolute, or God. It is a living energy whose vibration gives rise to the whole universe. Synonymous with the om sound and *pranava*, Omkar is the all-pervasive universal mantra. This one dynamic impulse reverberates within itself giving rise to all experience—intellectual, volitional, emotional, and spiritual. Omkar is also called *sat-chit-ananda*, Being-Consciousness-Bliss. The Absolute simply is—an eternally stable, self-luminous, conscious force continuously and joyously manifesting its own awareness. Satchitananda.

> The universe arises from sound. As do all things with form, from sound, form arises. (Sutra 92)

Exactly how this vibrant, self-aware, ever-pulsating ocean of pure consciousness manifests as our familiar material world is the subject of much scholarly debate. In general, all schema trace a hierarchical development beginning with the single Absolute that manifests in increasingly differentiated levels. Nityananda likewise sees the material world as the most differentiated and gross level. Because each successive level is contained within its more subtle predecessor, however, all things share certain basic elements that are the first and most subtle differentiations from the Absolute.

> When the life-energy moves in an outward direction, desires are born. There the mind follows, dividing and subdividing into the two-, four-, and six-fold properties of unconscious cosmic Nature and what we call "the world" comes into being. (Sutra 70)

Nityananda spoke primarily of two sets of such elements. In the first are the five categories of earth, water, fire, air, and ether. In the second set are the three primary *gunas* or constituent elements of cosmic Nature (*prakriti: sattva, rajas,* and *tamas*). Sattva is pure light and perfect balance. Tamas, at the other end of the spectrum, embodies inertia, darkness, and total density. Between the two lies Rajas—passion, fire, dynamic activity.

> All principles have a single root—the One Absolute, Parabrahma. (Sutra 5)

Omkar is the essence of them all; the "power of doership" of the Absolute, the essence of life, of words and objects, of human beings. Omkar is the heart of Atman, and Atman is central to the mystery of our essential nature—because Atman is the Self. In the sutras, a distinction is made between the individual Self (*jivatman*) and the divine Self (*paramatman*), a distinction that is only on the surface. The distinction is Maya. This does not mean that the world is an illusion. (After all, the power underlying everything is real power.) Rather, Maya implies that nothing outside and nothing inside is as it appears. Individual selves are not really separate. Instead they are like waves on the ocean's surface, each different but still water—only water. Likewise, any extension of the supreme Self is not different from the supreme Self. Jivatman is supreme conscious energy expressed as an individuated person, Paramatman is the Absolute, and they are both really the same thing. When Nityananda speaks of merging the Jivatman into the Paramatman, he is simply referring to the merging of ocean waves into water. Atman merging into Atman.

## The Nature of the Individual

> Sound arises in the inner sky of pure consciousness, the heart-space in the head, the sky of the heart. What manifests is Life-Power, the One. (Sutra 37)

Each individual reflects the structure of the universe. Whatever Divine Consciousness manifests in the universe, individuated consciousness manifests in the form of the human body. Nityananda used the words Omkar or Shakti when discussing the vitality of the Absolute. As this energy moves out from the source, it becomes distinct but not separate from the source. And as the essence of the individual Jivatman, it is called *kundalini*.

> Similarly, the life-force—Shakti, kundalini—is the same in all creatures, mobile and immobile. The sun and moon also are the same life-force. (Sutra 11)

Kundalini is the all-encompassing energy of life itself. In the individual human being, this single dynamic event manifests on three levels: biological, subtle or psychic, and purely spiritual. The energy of our biological existence is *prana-kundalini*. The energy that supports the intellectual and emotional manifestations of our being is *chitta-kundalini*, the mind. The third aspect, *para-kundalini*, is the condensed manifestation of pure consciousness; it is the same as Shakti, the same as Omkar. These aspects relate to different stages or states of consciousness. While they each manifest differently, their essence is the same *paramatman*. Awareness of this essence is liberation.

> Awaken the kundalini-shakti through the breath; for when it is roused, liberation is possible. (Sutra 20)

Prana-kundalini, or simply prana, is the driving force of our psycho-physical mechanism. It is the breath within the breath, the "breath of life." Not the same as the physical breath, prana is more accurately called the link between the mental and the physical. Thus, mind (*manas*) plays an important role in the unfoldment and expansion of the inner vision—because mind and breath are intimately related. The thoughts and feelings that arise and subside in the mind do so on the movement of this subtle breath of life. The practice of pranayama uses the mind to control prana while simultaneously using prana to control the mind. The aim of this practice is to bring the flow of subtle energy into the awareness and control of the individual.

> The three primary channels through which conscious creative energy circulates in the subtle body are the ida, the pingala, and the sushumna. Sushumna is the seat of kundalini. (Sutra 85)

This flow of energy takes place within a structure that is sometimes called the subtle body, with prana corresponding to the subtle breath. In the sutras, Nityananda speaks of the three primary nerves or *nadis*: the *ida*, the *pingala*, and the *sushumna*. They serve as channels in the subtle body for the flow of conscious energy and are arranged like the familiar medical symbol of the caduceus: a straight central channel (sushumna) flanked by two side channels (ida and pingala) that crisscross over the center like a loose braid. At each crossover point are centers called *chakras*, illustrated in the diagram.

> The subtle is in the chakras. In the subtle channels is the kundalini shakti—together they are Om. Realize and know the subtle. (Sutra 47)

A chakra is a point in time and space where various flows of energy interact and create a resonance that is uniquely different from the resonance of the individual energies that originally combined to make it. From these centers of vibration a human being's mental, emotional, and physical characteristics are determined and expressed.

> Just as severn chakras begin with the muladhara at the base of the spine... (Sutra 18)

There are seven major chakras, each corresponding to an area in the physical body: the base of the spine, the base of the sex organs, the navel, the heart, the throat, a point between the eyebrows, and the top of the head. Kundalini energy is said to lie dormant in the *muladhara*, the chakra at the base of the spine; the nadis also originate in the muladhara. In addition to the muladhara, Nityananda specifically refers to the *ajna* chakra between the eyebrows and the *sahasrara* chakra at the top of the head. The goal of yogic

The seven major chakras with their associated mystic symbols and Sanskrit letters.

practice is to rouse the sleeping kundalini, allowing it to rise through the nadis and chakras, finally to merge with the Absolute in the sahasrara chakra.

> The seat of such discrimination is in the sky of the heart. When the kundalini rises to this place in the head, then the breath is single and the universe is in one's Self. All is in the Self... (Sutra 42)

The sahasrara chakra at the top of the head is the seat of Self-realization. It is the junction point between the individual and the Divine, that point in a human being wherein lies the dynamic stillness that is the union of Shiva and Shakti. It is the only part of the psychobiological mechanism that is still, just as the hub of a wheel is still while the spokes and the rim move around it. It is the place from which all of the spiritual forces that make up a human being are extended, the place the breath comes from, the place the chakras come from, the place the physical body comes from.

> The Self is there before you and and it is there after you; even before you were born, there was creation. Only you are unaware. (Sutra 6)

A human being, then, is really an extension of a spiritual force. The dormant kundalini represents the furthest extension of that energy. As long as it is crystallized in this extension, the person is a limited being and sees things in terms of distinctions. When, through *shaktipat*, the kundalini begins to rise, this crystallization is loosened up. As the energy begins to flow again, it is reabsorbed into itself as the Divine.

> When the individual spirit leads the inner Shiva-Shakti upward to the Brahmarandhra at the top of the head, the individual becomes one with the Indivisible. This is liberation, indivisible liberation. (Sutra 16)

> Creation is nothing but energy released or projected from God. Entering back into it is dissolution. Identifying with the body is the cause of creation—as one sees it. Real dissolution takes place when the individual Self merges and dissolves in the Universal. (Sutra 25)

For Nityananda, the sahasrara chakra is synonymous with the Brahmarandhra, the point of dynamic stillness that equals the union of Shiva and Shakti. When the individual creative energy, in the form of kundalini, is re-awakened and merged into that point through the various yogic practices, the individual consciousness dissolves into universal consciousness. What manifests then is a complete state known as the divine inner Self. This is the state of universal consciousness and awareness of the Self as the source of the whole universe.

*Chidakasha* and *hridayakasha* refer to the awareness that arises in the state of divine consciousness. In that state we experience the inner as vast, maybe more vast than the whole external universe. Hridayakasha means "heart-space;" the heart referred to is the essence or the heart of the whole universe. Chidakasha is consciousness-space, the sky of consciousness, or "the sky of the heart." The heart-space in the head, the sky of the heart, the Brahmarandhra—these all refer to the same experience of infinite expansiveness.

> The source of liberation is Shiva. The linga in the head is Shiva. It is all Om. (Sutra 13)

This Brahmarandhra is also referred to in Nityananda's sutras as the *linga* in the head, which is the symbol of Shiva. In Indian temples, the linga is a stone or metal object said to have a masculine quality, to be completely passive, and to contain the whole universe within itself. It arose as a symbol of Shiva because the linga in the head is the abode of Shiva—the source of all that is.

## The Process of Liberation

Within a human being there is a vast reservoir of spiritual knowledge and pure capability, yet this great treasure is rarely tapped. Our involvement in the world and our entanglement in the struggle for survival limit our awareness to desires and their objects. Like a kaleidoscope, these desires are continuously changing form; the subtle images of shape and color never allow us to really grasp what we think we are seeing. Unless we recognize the kaleidoscope for the illusion it is, much unhappiness and frustration can result.

> Return to the Self within and know your own secret! The universe is inside you and you are inside the universe. The inner Self is the One dancing in all... (Sutra 65)

The primary paradox of unity and diversity recurs at every level. While the process of liberation appears hierarchical at first glance, the orderly image of a ladder of ever-higher levels breaks down on close scrutiny. The process is really more like drawing a series of ever-expanding concentric circles. *Jiva* is in the center and the Absolute is in the outermost circle as well as the paper on which it lies and the pen with which it is drawn. This is a paradox that cannot be neatly resolved through language. Only by continuous and deep contemplation can the nature of this paradox be penetrated and encompassed. What follows is called liberation.

> Sound arises in the inner sky of pure consciousness, the heart-space in the head, the sky of the heart. What manifests is Life-Power, the One. (Sutra 37)

Nityananda addressed this paradox indirectly through the image of the heart-space in the head, the chidakash, the sky of the heart. This verbal image brings together what is "above" and what is "below" with intuitive clarity; in the sky of consciousness, there is no duality and no paradox. The question then is how to reach this center. Nityananda directs the seeker to "the royal road."

> A true guru can turn you from the jungle road of ignorance to the royal road of spiritual knowledge. (Sutra 102)

> But without the Guru, you cannot reach the goal. (Sutra 9)

The paradox is repeated in the form of the guru, because the guru has two aspects. Nityananda called these the primary (or action) guru and the secondary (or causal) guru. On the one hand, there is the physical teacher. This is a personality to be dealt with and talked to, a person who performs actions that have an effect in the world, a person viewed by some with admiration and by others with disgust; in other words, someone viewed by ordinary people as the same or less than they are. On the other hand, for the few people who are able to, or care to, look deeply into the situation, what is really there is not a personality but an extraordinary field of spiritual energy from which they can draw nourishment for their innermost being. With this nourishment, they can attain complete maturity in the supreme state of pure consciousness.

> The secondary guru leads you to the well—the primary
> guru drinks from it. (Sutra 104)

The physical aspect of the guru, the secondary teacher,
serves as a doorway. Through our diligence, love, and devotion we pass through this doorway of the physical teacher
into the level of consciousness that Nityananda calls the
action guru. The action guru is the same as Parabrahma,
Paramashiva, or chidakasha. At this level, we express the
infinite spaciousness, extraordinary power, and creative
intelligence that are characteristics of the essential state of
unity from which all experience takes its form.

> Liberation does not come searching for you. You must
> make the effort to seek it. (Sutra 117)

The effort required if you sincerely seek God is to see
through the form, to pass beyond the personality, the indi-
viduality, and the eccentricity of the teacher, and in so
doing to transcend your own personality and limitations.

> Draw the breath up to the Brahmarandhra at the top of
> the head. Kindle the fire, purify the subtle channels,
> burn up the impurities. This is the yoga-fire of deliber-
> ation... The pure energy of the Supreme. (Sutra 28)

The power inherent in the presence of the guru energizes
every level of a human being. The transmission of this

power is *shaktipat*, the transmission or descent of grace. Shaktipat brings about a quantum leap in awareness that puts us in contact with the innate freedom and spontaneous creative power that is eternally and everywhere present as the source of all. It awakens the deepest potentiality within us, and the kundalini shakti begins its extraordinary unfoldment. As this unfoldment continues, the entire structure of the human being is refined and purified. When subjected to fire, iron is freed of its gross crystallization and impurities and reorganized as the finer, stronger metal of steel. The human being also, through contact with the forge of the guru, becomes purified by the inner fire of kundalini and is established in the supreme state of awareness. Seeing past the form of the physical teacher brings awareness of the power that is functioning as and through the teacher. And stilling the mind in the flow of that power is liberation.

> First silence the mind and establish it in the Self, then concentrate deeply with spiritual discernment. (Sutra 179)

When the various waves of creative energy that form the mind are stilled and become like the surface of a calm lake, our awareness can penetrate our own depth and recognize the complete oneness of our individual Self and the Divine. Deep contact or connection with a guru enables us to feel so deeply secure and calm that we can begin to turn within and observe the workings of our inner universe without the doubts, fears, and tensions that continuously draw the mind of the ordinary person back into the realm of dualistic awareness.

> Mind is the root of bondage and liberation, of good and evil, of sin and holiness. (Sutra 71)

The mind is both the entity to be stilled and the means of stilling it, for the nature of the mind is complex. Nityananda used many different terms to distinguish its facets. The major distinction is between *manas* and *buddhi*. Manas is the ordinary limited mind and buddhi is the higher mind, the one capable of subtle discrimination and spiritual discernment. In some classical Indian systems, the word *chitta* denotes the whole mental apparatus composed of three parts: manas (the perceiving mind), buddhi (the discriminating mind), and ego ("I-consciousness"). Nityananda used "body-idea" and "body-consciousness" synonymously with "I-consciousness." Although simple thoughts, feelings, and desires arise in the mind, the mind is also capable of realizing *jnana* and truth. Jnana is the highest wisdom, the wisdom of the *jnani*, one who has realized the Self. Here again is a paradox, for the wisest person has transcended the mind and its desires. "A jnani has no mind," says Nityananda.

> Without a pure mind, how can you develop equal vision? Without practice, how can you develop balance?

Through practice, the subtle intelligence develops and the desire for objects disappears. (Sutra 141)

As our understanding expands and we begin to see beyond the "body-idea" and beyond the limits of ordinary mind, a sense of detachment also grows. Detachment, desirelessness, and perfect dispassion for worldliness (what Nityananda called *vairagya*) are necessary requirements for the seeker. The Sanskrit word *sannyasi* means "renunciate", literally "one who has cast away." However, renunciation is a subtle concept. It is not objects that we must renounce, but our desire for objects; not actions, but our attachment to the results of those actions. True renunciation is not of things but of the desire for things. Vairagya is the attitude leading to a state of understanding in which the true nature of objects is known. Consequently, these objects no longer have any power over a person.

> No need to strive for anything. When the mind chases desires, one must strive to attain one-pointedness. Concentrate the mind in the higher mind... (Sutra 80)

Meditation is an integral part of *sadhana*. Nityananda spoke of meditation as a focused concentration, the merging of mind into wisdom, the look within. The goal is bringing the mind to perfect one-pointedness; achieving this goal tests all faculties of the seeker. The mind must be stilled and drawn away from desire; the breath must be harmonious and ultimately become single; the awareness must reach inside to come in touch with and observe the action of the kundalini shakti.

> Like milk being boiled, the vital breath in the sushumna channel is heated by intense faith and discrimination and led toward the sahasrara chakra, the still point at the top of the head. As the kundalini power crosses each subtle energy center, properties of the energy that evolves as the world change. (Sutra 21)

Then, as a natural result of the awakening of the inner transforming power, the kundalini shakti rises through the chakras to join and merge into the heart-space, the Brahmarandhra. The love and happiness that then arise within us dissolve all the various tensions and superficial desires and satisfy our deepest needs. With a full heart, the mind can become still and one-pointed on the power of the Divine Presence. This is the merging of the individual into the universal and transcendent that Nityananda consistently called the most important purpose of our presence on this earth. To merge heart to heart and spirit to spirit with the guru in the field of supreme Shiva-Shakti frees a human being from all mechanistic thinking and from the bonds of cause and effect. This is the union of the individual and the Divine.

> Fulfillment is possible only when you merge with this
> pure heart. There all idea of "you" and "I" disappears.
> In the sky of the heart is liberation, love, and devotion.
> (Sutra 40)

Liberation is the clear, luminous recognition that our mind, emotions, and physical body are nothing more than extensions of the supreme Mantra of God that pulsates silently everywhere and always at once. Everywhere we look, inside and outside, we experience nothing but the extraordinary clarity, beauty, and power of the supreme Self. It is eternally pulsating, creating, absorbing, and manifesting yet again—ourselves, the world, all that is. This is simply the fundamental expression of its absolute freedom to do whatever it wants, an expression of its supreme freedom and its incredible joy. Satchitananda!

## Conclusion

In all places and in every age, there are many good people who seek spirituality, who have spiritual understanding, and who have some positive concerns for humanity. Yet in any age there are only a few people, rare and great beings indeed, who can communicate the highest transcendent state of consciousness to other human beings and who dwell in that state while still functioning in this world as ordinary—and possibly eccentric—human beings.

Nityananda was such a rare and gifted being. And because he spoke from a state of complete Self-awareness, his spiritual presence flows through his words. By becoming aware of the ongoing pulsation and remaining aware of it every day, the mind itself becomes a mantra. Whatever is spoken in that state is sacred, pure, and uplifting. In that state, the sounds that come and the way they are articulated and joined to form images is something mysterious and magical, a manifestation of the freedom of our innate, pure consciousness. Nityananda's words came from that state. They inspire us to open our minds and hearts to the extraordinary creative energy that permeates our lives, and to experience, recognize, and appreciate the miracles that happen to us.

Nityananda always said, "When the disciple calls with love, I am there." For people who are willing to open their eyes and hearts, Nityananda is a symbol of the enduring, ever-present power of the Divine in the world. This dynamic spiritual presence has the power to transform lives, to relieve suffering, to grant freedom from poverty and disease, and most importantly, from hard-heartedness. When you are filled with this power, then even in the most simple circumstances life becomes an experience of complete fulfillment and happiness. Our lives become an act of service expressed in a state of detachment. As we begin directing our lives toward the recognition of that supreme creative power that is our essence, then we speak, think, and act from that power. Our lives are in perfect harmony, perfect balance, perfect union with the power of Life.

Nityananda felt that such a life of perfect union was possible for everyone. This is perhaps what impresses me most about these sutras—the simple and total availability of that supreme state to anyone who sincerely seeks it. The goal of Nityananda's teaching, and the single most important thing each of us can do with our lives, is to recognize the creative power within us and dissolve the mind into it. It is clear from these sutras that for Nityananda, this supreme, highest state is neither the privilege of special birth nor the exclusive property of some special class of beings. It is available to everyone. The simple purity, the joy, and the extraordinary communion with the Divine that are the outstanding characteristics of Nityananda's life and presence are accessible to everyone: to me and to you.

Thousands of people, sometimes tens of thousands in a day, had the opportunity to experience and participate in the Divine Presence that was Nityananda. Yet how many people took away something great and enduring from it? Not nearly as many as were there. But Nityananda made it accessible to everyone—there were no barriers. Thus, it is up to each of us. Through our devotion, love, and diligence, we can grow in our understanding of that simple and perfectly full state that is the field of our individual life and the field of all experience.

The greatest treasure in the whole world is hidden inside each of us. And while we may never be successful in the worldly sense, this treasure we can definitely find. Seeking that treasure is a good thing—but finding it is better.

It is up to you.

*Swami Chetanananda*

# THE SELF
*atman*

Nityananda always urged devotees to look inward for the Truth. He said that the best place for pilgrimage along "the royal road to liberation" was in the heart. Even in demonstrations of respect, he stressed the internal, saying that devotion offered from the *sthana* (literally "the place," implying the heart) always reached him. Once, wishing to show her respect to Nityananda, a woman began to roll on the floor from the ashram entrance to where he sat. As she proceeded, he said, "This is not necessary. Is it chapati dough? Why roll like that? What is to be rolled up is not the body but the mind and the senses."

In 1929 two young women from Mangalore went to Kanhangad in search of Nityananda. There was only one train in the morning and one in the evening between the two towns. The young women searched for the Master all day but could not find him, even though they went most of the way to what is now known as Guruvan. They were making their disappointed return when they suddenly saw Nityananda perched on a tree. They told him they did not know anything about spiritual matters but had come for guidance. "It is the spark, the spark," he repeated from the tree. "Blow on it until it is a blazing fire." Then he added,

"Go now or you will miss the train." This message sufficed to guide the women, devotees from that time onward.

When Nityananda was asked by a member of the local legislature to define "grace of the guru" (*guru-kripa*), he  responded with the following questions: Where is your hometown? How long does it take to get there by road? By sea? By rail? After the man replied, Nityananda asked him how long the trip would take by air. The legislator said that it would take less that thirty minutes. "Grace of the guru is like air travel," Nityananda said, "providing the shortest and fastest way to the place of our origin in the Infinite."

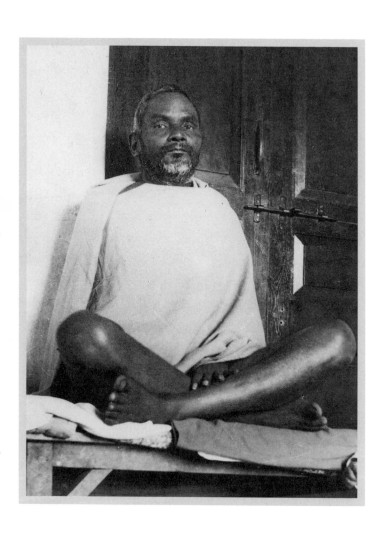

1

The real sunrise is in the sky of the heart;
It is the best one.
Just as the water jar reflects the sun,
So the entire universe shines
In the heart-space of the Self.
When you are in a train, the whole world
Appears to pass by.
Similarly, the whole universe can be known
Within the Self.*

 2

The universal Self is in the individual Self.
Just so, liberation comes from recognizing
The subtle in the gross,
The unity in diversity,
The similarity in differences,
The truth in untruth,
The light in darkness,
The life in death.
This is real liberation.

---

*An asterisk at the end of a sutra indicates further information
 can be found in the commentary.

3

Know your real Self.
A true yogi, a true sannyasi, has conquered
The mind;
He or she has no mind.
If you enter a dark room after looking at the
Bright sun,
What do you see?
Nothing.
Look at the Self with the inner eye
And you will see the Self
Everywhere.

 4

When you get hungry,
You know it.
Everything is known to the Self.

5

All principles have a single root—
The One Absolute, Parabrahma.
To know this principle is
Liberation in this lifetime.

You must see the river at its source—
Not after it merges with the sea.
You must see the central root of the tree
For all trees have only one central root.
All have only one God.
To see all with equal vision is
Liberation in this lifetime.

6

Why do you hold an umbrella?
For protection from the rain.
The illusion of duality is the rain—Maya,
Truth is the umbrella,
And a steadfast mind is the handle.
Truth is in everything but few people realize it.

Maya, the cosmic power responsible for our
Sense of duality, comes from the Self—
The Self does not come from Maya.
The prime minister is under the king,
But he is not the king.
The mind is not the Self—
It is a reflection of the Self.
The mind is two grades below the Self.
The mind has an end,
But the Self has no end.
The mind is often deluded,
But the Self is not deluded. and not subject
To the three forms of manifest reality—

The dense, the dynamic, the still.
Such qualities apply only to the mind.
The mind is to the Self
As the river is to the sea.

The Self is the sea, its water measureless.
The Self is without beginning or end.
The Self does not come and it does not go.
Wherever you turn, it is there.
Nothing else is seen.
The Self is there before you and it is there
After you;
Even before you were born, there was creation.
Only you are unaware.*

7

To search elsewhere for what you already
Hold in your hand is fruitless.
If you light a lamp on the top floor of
Your house and then close all the doors,
No light will be visible below.
"Watch the movies!" "See the drama!"—
From the head, we mean.
Everything can be seen from one place.
It is unnecessary to go to different places
To see different things.
You can see the city of Madras from here
As well as from there.
But it is better to see it from one place;
See the form in the head.


The heart is not below the neck—it is above it!
As we cook, the fire's flames rise.
In the same way does the heart above
Fill with light.
There is no darkness here.
Beheaded, a person is not easily recognized;
One must look at the face.

The heart sees through the eyes,
And you must have inner sight.
The sky of the heart, the heart-space,
Is nothing other than the triangle-shaped face.
Recognize a person by looking at the face.
Know your own secret.
Know your Self.

 8

Just as we see a reflection of the sky
In a vessel's still water,
So we see the sky of consciousness
With the inner eye.

9

If God is in you and you are in God,
Then creation and dissolution—Maya—
Dissolves in the Self.
For those free of the world's bondage,
There is no forgetting the Self.
One who knows that we are not the body has
Eternal bliss.
The Self is free of ideas of honor or dishonor;
One who gives up these ideas has reached
The goal and attained peace.
In the infinite there is nothing finite,
But without the guru, you cannot reach the goal.

10

For the person firmly established in the One,
There is no rebirth.
For such a person, free of desires,
Death comes only as he or she wills.

To see the One is subtle;
To see the One is to see the same Self in all.
This is "same-sightedness," equal vision.
Seeing the One in all by looking inward.
Seeing that this world and the next world are
One,
The union of the individual Self and
The Absolute.

The individual is the modification of the mind,
The Absolute is the great silence:
Beyond qualities,
Neither good nor evil,
Neither hot nor cold,
Formless, free of qualities,
No-thing.

## 11

If you have come to buy milk,
Why ask the price of the cow?
If you seek the Self,
Why be concerned about the body?
One who has attained the Self is in the body
But like the dry kernel in the coconut
Is not attached to it.
A rope burnt to ashes cannot be used to tie.
No man can harm another—
Each does it to himself with his own thinking.
A boatman is needed to push the barge across
The river, and a guru is needed for initiation.
Once the opposite bank is reached,
The boatman's help is not needed.
The boat in the water is like the Self in the body.
If your feet are muddy,
You look for water to wash them.
But if you are afraid to touch the water,
The mud will remain.
One hand alone makes no sound,
But two hands coming together make

Sound-energy.
Your fingers are not the same size, yet when
Scooping water, they become one.
When there is experience, it is One.
All holy men and perfect ones are alike.
All water in the well is the same—
There are not two kinds.
Similarly, the life-force—Shakti, kundalini—
Is the same in all creatures,
Mobile and immobile.
The sun and moon also
Are the same life-force.

The Self in the heart-sky
And the heart-sky in the Self are One.
Those who know this One sing in ecstasy!
They know the bliss-producing kundalini.
They discover their own life-force
And awaken it;
Join with it.
By joining with it repeatedly,
They attain devotion and liberation.
They conquer birth,

They conquer death and its brood,
They forget all.
Know the true nature of Maya;
Likewise know the nature of eternal bliss.
O mind, become one with eternal bliss.
Drink of the Self in the head;
Unite the world with the Self in the head
For here is the fulfillment of birth.
Strive for the Self in the head.
In the Self, unite the three states of
Wakefulness, dreams, and sleep.
Keep the key of the higher mind close at hand.
As you guard the key to a treasure, carefully
Keep subtle discrimination in the head.
Water is hot only if it is left on the fire—
On the ground it becomes cool.
Let the higher mind be like water kept warm.
Faith must be constant.
The embodied Self is like a calf confined,
Always eager to escape.
So is the individual Self eager to escape to
Higher wisdom.

12

Unite meditation, mind, and faith at the
Point of potentiality—
Contracting and ready to create.
Merge in the center between the eyebrows
And attain oneness.
Following the path of discrimination,
Firmly fix the pure mind in Om—
The universal sound.
Steady the mind by practicing
Pure concentration;
Become one-pointed.
Only by being totally absorbed in the Self,
Can we establish our state of consciousness
In the Infinite.
Enter the sky of the heart!
See! The world has no separate existence.
Be free of this idea of the body!
To hold firmly onto consciousness is
Difficult without practicing
Spiritual discipline.

To those established in the Self,
The body is foreign;
The gross and the subtle are like
The fruit and its seed.
To those established in "I am not the body,"
Union with the Absolute is not
Something separate.
It is all Samadhi, always Samadhi,
Absolute Samadhi,
Mind-surpassing Samadhi.

To one submerged in the sweetness of
Universal wisdom,
The sweetness is not something separate.
The external world has no importance.

## 13

The source of liberation is Shiva.
The linga in the head is Shiva.
It is all Om.
Enlightenment is the most important thing.
Without channels for the flow
Of subtle breath in the body,
There is no sound.

Love and devotion are the oil,
The channel is the wick,
Discrimination is the lantern.
Flame, light, and glass are the channels;
The air hole is the Brahmarandhra,
The still point at the top of the head.
The form of discrimination is intelligence.*

14

Yes, Pilgrim,
Shiva is in Kashi, the ancient City of Light.
But Kashi is the sky of the heart.
The mind is Kashi, everything is Kashi,
The eternal Self is Kashi—and it is in the head.
The ten sounds are eternal.
Find the subtle Kashi in the silence of the mind.

The city of Haridwar is the body's nine gates.
It is in the sky of the heart.
The heart is the seat of peace.
—Perform yajna, the ritual sacrifice, and
Awaken the inner fire of kundalini.
Taste the nectar of spiritual wisdom.
The only effective pilgrimage is the
Inner journey!*

— 15

Cleverness is like traveling on foot.
A clever person will wander,
For the mind is fickle.
Shakti is the power that enters the heart.
And so, the spiritual life is like
Traveling by train.

The body is the train, the mind is the passenger.
Without passengers, the train will not move,
Tickets are not issued, people do not gather.
There is no first class, no second, no third.
Mind is the peace class,
Subtle discrimination is the engineer,
The head is the engine,
The nerves and subtle channels are the gears
Through which the breath of life moves.*

_16_

Praise Shiva!
When the individual spirit leads
The inner Shiva-Shakti upward
To the Brahmarandhra at the top of the head,
The individual becomes one with the
Indivisible.
This is liberation, indivisible liberation,
The bliss of the Absolute.
Pure consciousness.

In the beginning was Shiva,
In the beginning was Shiva-Shakti alone.
The great protector is eternal bliss.
Great desirelessness is eternal bliss.
You who are without desire,
You who are without the three gunas,
You who are endowed with virtue,
Master of your Self, king of Jivanmukti—
Look inside!

The human form is the highest of creatures.
There is nothing higher.
It has created all the countries.*

17

There are three important channels
In the subtle body.
Sushumna is the sun channel in the center,
Ida is the moon channel on the left, and
Pingala is the star channel on the right.
In color, the sun nadi is red,
The moon nadi is blue, and
The star nadi is green.
They join in the sky of the heart.

In time, the Om sound is heard in the head.
This sound, though truly one and undivided,
Can manifest as many—
The roar of the sea,
Notes of the flute, violin, or harmonium,
Beating of drums or bells, even
The buzzing of bees.
These are the ten sounds of the
One subtle sound, indivisible.*

18

The centers of conscious energy below the neck
Relate to hatha yoga.
Control over these chakras is acquired
By controlling the universal life-force
In the intense practice of Pranayama.
The centers above the neck relate to raja yoga.
Control over these chakras is acquired through
The practice of meditation.

Just as seven chakras begin with the muladhara
At the base of the spine,
So in raja yoga seven chakras lie above the neck.
Beginning at the throat chakra,
The kundalini—Shiva's creative power—must rise.

The fruit grows at the top of the coconut tree:
Likewise the fruit of divine wisdom
Is experienced in the brain
At the top of the spinal cord.*

19

The head is the mango;
Within it lies the essence of the five senses.
This sweet ambrosia
Is the supreme energy in man!

 20

Awaken the kundalini Shakti
Through the breath.
For when it is roused, liberation is possible.
Faith holds the rope of vital breath—
And onto this rope you must hold tightly!
Bind faith with the rope of
One-pointed concentration,
For what is perfect concentration but faith?
Keep your attention constantly on it.
Join steadfast faith to perfect concentration and
Faith will fill every nerve of your body.

For one with perfect concentration,
There is no separate thing called "Maya".
The mind itself is Maya.
The mind creates all forms.

All matter, all relationships, all cause and effect,
Light, the universe—
All arise from the mind, from Maya.
The moment this is realized,
All fear of Maya disappears.
In meditation, remember your real form.
Stabilize the mind in the practice of meditation
And concentrate consciousness in
The sky of the heart.
This is liberation!

The path to liberation is not far from the Self.
Sin and merit are as close as is the eye to the ear.
It is not beyond the higher mind,
Not beyond subtle discernment
Where pleasure and pain are one.
The Way of Buddhi leads to liberation.
To steady the mind in one's Self,
To be one-minded,
This is liberation.

All wisdom is in the Self.
In the beginning,
Wisdom is something to be known.

Later, wisdom dissolves in the Self where there is

Nothing to be said and

Nothing to be heard.

It is the state of Nothingness,

The state called "Shunya".

The subtle breath is like a rope:

Whether it is moving in or moving out,

The movement is the same—

Indivisible and unaffected by time.

Only when entangled with the physical nature

Are there differences.

Only when engrossed in the different properties

Of the world

Does one forget his true nature.

With the help of the higher mind

A person can take an upward course!

Steadied by the rope of faith,

The subtle breath turns upward toward liberation,

Toward freedom from sense-objects.

Then comes peace.


Reach for that peace!

Live in this world and in the next world.

This is Being-Consciousness-Bliss—
Satchitananda!
Such a person is eternally free,
Free of attachment to the results of work,
Free of bondage,
Eternally one-minded.
Until the ego-sense of separateness
Is dissolved,
Liberation is indeed far off.
Without the sense of One,
There is no yoga, there is no freedom.
Only in union and in oneness is there real yoga,
Free of all desires and all delusion.
This is the path to liberation.
Doubt will not disappear until you realize
Oneness within.
If you see something you do not like,
You call it madness—
But if you like it,
You do not call it madness…

The mind is like a piece of cotton whipped
By the wind;

Devotion is like water poured on the cotton

To steady it.

So is the mind steadied.

Wetted with the water of wisdom,

Consciousness is fixed.

This is liberation.

It is possible to meditate on the Self

Even while doing other things

Because the objects of the senses are

Outside us, not inside.

It is possible to keep the higher mind separate—

But if the driver takes his hands off

The wheel, the car runs anywhere

And creates danger.

Fix the mind in the Buddhi—

Do not let it wander.

Practice inner meditation and

Develop the power of introspection.

O mind, enter the sky of consciousness!

Develop subtle discernment and fill every

Nerve of the body with it.

O mind, always be content—

And not deluded by shadows!*

## 21

The subtle kundalini is comprehended
By following the path of the higher mind.
Like milk being boiled,
The vital breath in the sushumna channel is
Heated by intense faith and discrimination
And led toward the sahasrara chakra,
The still point at the top of the head.
As the kundalini power
Crosses each subtle energy center,
Properties of the energy that evolves
As the world change.
And as they change—so does one's whole birth.
As the breath of life
Abiding in the chakras as enlightenment
Moves upward,
Peace and patience flower.

Cross the five centers, the five houses,
And reach the *ajna* chakra between the eyebrows.
Freed from the six gunas,
Enter that highest state—
Being-Consciousness-Bliss!

Enter the fire-circle
In the inner sky of the heart
Where Shiva and Shakti merge and play,
Where past, present, and future merge
To come together in the *bindu*.
In this undifferentiated point
Find the fire of spiritual wisdom.
Meditate on this fire.
Attain the seat of consciousness in the head.
Let the vital breath unite with Shiva and
Dance as the one Self.
Conquer mantra and yantra,
The symbols spoken and the symbols drawn.

Let the higher mind rise
To the center of the sky of consciousness
And become one with the dawn of the Self.
Offer up the body's properties and actions
And let your spirit merge with the absolute Self.
Seat your spirit at the sushumna channel's crest,
Its real home.
Let the sense of "mine" and "yours" merge.
Let all properties of the individual be unified,

Become a Perfected One and fear nothing.
Knowing the way to the Absolute,
Give of this food to others.
Conquer birth and death;
Be free of them and enjoy eternal peace.
The light of the higher mind
Reveals all strengths and weaknesses,
All workings of the mind.
Like the sky and its reflection,
The natural and the subtle are seen separately
By those who have realized the Self.

The inner state is like a jug immersed in water.
All is water.
Be immersed in the waters of wisdom,
Let the waters of the Self wash desires
From the mind.
Find joy!
Enter liberation!
Mind, remain always on the path of liberation—
Whether walking, sitting, standing, or sleeping.
Liberation entertains no rules of time
Even in the midst of crowds,

Let your inner being remain in
The sky of consciousness.
With intense faith, lead the mind
To drink of liberation.
Devotion and liberation are one:   *Bakti*
Become one with the power and sound of Om.

 22

The fruit is according to inner faith.
Good and evil do not apply to the Self,
Which is like a mirror that reflects the form
That the mind creates.
The individual Self is like a bird in the nest—
When the nest breaks down,
The bird simply flies away.
Depending on its efforts,
It may build a new nest
In minutes, months, or years.
From here, you can reach the railway station
In an hour or in a month.

23

Creation dissolves into the breath of life,
Vayu, prana, vital-force, blue in color.

Practice raja yoga and experience
The bliss of the Indivisible Absolute.
Enter into the One! Dissolve the many!

24

To bring your creative energy under control—
Breathe.
Samadhi is the upward breath, the God within.
With the upward breath established,
You will find the entire universe inside.
In all creatures the upward breath is the same.

The raja yogi is at one with this
Infinite movement
Whether sitting, talking, standing, walking.
Raja yoga is the highest yoga.
It is like climbing to the roof of a building
And looking below.
When intellect and wisdom are united,

You will know complete peace,
Formless and without qualities.

Bliss has no qualities.
This state is called jivanmukti—
Knowing liberation while alive!
Self-Realization.

 25

In raja yoga there are no holy works to perform.
No rituals, no holiness in a particular place.
Spiritual discipline consists of regulating
The breath through the chakras.
Respect and love offered from the highest chakra
Reach the entire universe.

Creation is nothing but energy
Released or projected from God.
Entering back into it is dissolution.
Identifying with the body is the cause
of creation—as one sees it.
Real dissolution takes place
When the individual Self
Merges and dissolves in the Universal.

26

As air is pumped into a bicycle tire,
So the body's subtle channels are filled
By thoughts on higher knowledge.
First the channels must be cleansed,
Then the prana is drawn up,
Step by step,
To the Brahmarandhra in the center of the brain.

Merge with the Supreme Self,
Join in the "Divine Sport."
Mind and intelligence merge into the Self
And become wisdom.
Drink from the well of eternal joy and penetrate
The nectar's core.
Who is it, anyway, who is eternally blissful?
Uncover the secret of God's delight—
Awaken the kundalini Shakti!

Like a child rocked to sleep
In a cradle,
Gather the thoughts in the head
And churn them into a swing.

Supreme delight!
Eternal bliss!
Enter the Shiva linga in the head.

 27

Mind, enter the mansion of bliss!
When flood waters cover everything,
The wells and tanks are lost beneath them.
Because of darkness, light is revealed.
When you taste the sweet, remember
The pungent.
What is the state of the individual who
Realizes that the body is not
The Self?
Such a person has regained the original state
Of purity.

"I" and "mine" are invisible to the physical eye;
They do not exist above the tip of the nose.
That which is above these has
No beginning and no end.
What is seen with the physical eye has both
Beginning and end.

The Self is invisible to the physical eye;
It has no beginning and no end,
It is ever constant.
The power of the Self is impossible to lessen!

The Self, like space, is the same in all directions.
The head is the abode of light
With the brilliance of millions of suns.
Which is bigger—the eye or the sun?
If the eye is damaged, is it possible to see the sun?
The eye is more important.
The form of images is a creation of the mind.
A photograph reflects the body of
The sitter—not the virtue or lack of virtue
Of the photographer.

 28

Seeing all equally is the upward breath at the
Time of death.
Equal-sightedness is the divine sight:
Indivisible, full of delight,
Subtle, eternal.
Yoga is balancing the incoming and

Outgoing breaths.
With the guru's grace, cultivate this balance—
Meditate in the head,
Meditate on the ocean of eternal delight,
Meditate on the ida, the pingala, and the
Sushumna channels.
Arise, kundalini-delight!

The match is in the box, the light is in the match.
Strike the match and light the fire!
Ignorance is darkness, knowledge is light—
But kundalini is the eternal delight.
Kundalini is the eternal delight in the heart,
The "Light of Brahma"
Ablaze with the light of a million suns.
Sunlight is the subtle light,
The solar nerve is the sushumna channel,
The lunar nerve is the ida, and
The stellar nerve is the pingala.

The essence of the third eye is spiritual wisdom.
In this channel of wisdom is deep sleep;
There is no wakefulness.

Balancing the inward and the outward breath,
Enjoy the subtle sleep.
Find the eternal joy of the balanced breath.
The seat of the breath is the truth,
The inward space,
Unbounded pure awareness,
The sky of the heart.
Within this space is the tower of
Eternal delight—
The seat of peace!

Sleep consciously;
Not the gross sleep of the beast,
But the sleep of man,
Sleep the spiritual sleep—
When talking, when sitting,
Without thoughts, without desires, without ideas.
Fix your attention on the breath,
Listen to the inward and outward breath,
The sacred sound.
Do this with constant ardent devotion and
Love for God and attain liberation.

Draw the breath up and down,
As if drawing water from the well.
The upward-drawn breath is the inhalation.
The breath suspended in between is
The "real seat."
The downward breath is the exhalation.

Draw the breath up to the Brahmarandhra
At the top of the head.
Kindle the fire,
Purify the subtle channels,
Burn up the impurities.
This is the yoga-fire of deliberation,
The fire of digestion,
The solar light,
The pure energy of the Supreme.
The entire universe is this pure energy.
Creation is but a delusion of the mind—
There is no creation to the equal-sighted.

29

The Self is not perceived by the physical eye
But by the mind;
It is not something with form or properties.
Those who identify with the physical body
Find it difficult to see the Self.
Turn your attention from the visible and
Intensify your awareness of the invisible.
As long as the mind dwells on the visible world,
It will see both pain and pleasure.
But the invisible world holds
Neither pain nor pleasure.

 30

Good and evil merge into the one Self
As all rivers ultimately flow into the sea.
Good and evil arise from the Self
And return to that from which they came.
Offer all up to the Self!

31

Only when you see the sunrise in the sky of
The heart can you describe it.
But you must see it in yourself.
If your mind and intellect are one with the Self,
You can describe it.
But if they are separate,
It is not possible.
The higher mind, what is called
"Subtle discrimination" or "spiritual discernment,"
Is the union of intelligence and spiritual wisdom.

The sun reflected in water is unsteady.
So also the mind is fickle when it is
Caught in Maya.
This is delusion! This is madness!
Regardless of what you eat,
The way to the stomach is the same.
Regardless of a letter's contents,
The postbox is the same.
It is the tongue that distinguishes between
Sweet and salt—

To the mind there is no difference.
Just as you cage a bird and tie its legs
Before teaching it to speak,
Cage the intelligence in the mind
And learn the One.

 3 2

Without purifying the mind,
There is no contentment.
Without purifying the mind,
There is no steadiness of mind,
No liberation from words.
Just as ice and water soon become one,
So a person who realizes the Self
Becomes one with it.
Just as rivers merge into the sea,
So desires and impressions merge in the Self.

The Self is not an object.
Karma, the force of past action, is an object.
Look at a ship in the sea:
Ship and water appear to be one but they are
Really separate.

Be like the ship!
Have no attachment to worldly things.
As priests impatiently wait for the table to be set
And the meal served,
So you should wait for purification and liberation.

 33

Once you attain perfect inner peace, there is
No need to travel anywhere.
No need to see anything.
No need for pilgrimages to holy places.
All can be seen within.

Coming and going are simply the mind's delusions.
True peace, true liberation is attained
When the one Self in all is seen.
This is liberation from bondage,
This is desirelessness.
If you are looking for the object held in
Your hand,
Look in your hand—not elsewhere!
So with all things:
Test them within.

34

Like a bird with clipped wings,
Let the ten senses be restrained in service to
The higher mind.
Draw the life-force from the ten directions
Into one path;
Draw it inward and upward to the sky of the heart.
Find inner peace.
Find liberation in equal-sightedness.
From the heart of freedom, see all as free.

The body is the engine, knowledge is the steam,
Discrimination is the movement, faith is the rail.
Let the train be guided correctly.
The higher mind is the driver,
The digestive system is the boiler,
The subtle energy channels are the gears.
Enter the Self through the path of wisdom
And attain peace!

35

The Self is not perceived by the senses
But by the organs of knowledge,
By spiritual wisdom.
It is separate from the physical body.
Yogis who know the true nature of the senses and
Live by that knowledge are great and
Realized souls—
What they speak is wisdom.
The tamarind fruit is sticky to the touch;
But great souls are like the tamarind seed,
Pure and immaculate.
Their hearts are eternally young.

## 36

Only constant practice makes the state of
Perfect desirelessness steady and
Permanent.
It is not related to the body.
With the mind fixed and unwavering,
Then one sees the Self.
When both wisdom and divine wisdom
Are transcended,
Then one sees the Self.
When one knows but is as if one does not know,
Then one sees the Self.

Those who see the Self are
Like the blind though they see,
Like the deaf though they hear.
Their actions are like inaction.
Though their senses are functioning,
They are not attached to them;
They tend toward dissolution
And away from creation.
Their capacity to forget is great.

They concentrate on the fruit of the
Coconut—not on its shell;
On the Self—not on the body.

Those who see the Self are
Beyond merit and demerit.
Differing like a boat from its surrounding water.
Like the gross from the subtle.
Indifferent to bodily functions,
They concentrate only on divine wisdom
As if drinking the juice of the sugarcane and
Discarding the stalk.
Once converted to sugar,
The juice cannot become cane again.
Once the Self has been realized,
The body-idea never returns.
Like old vessels renewed by repairs and polish,
When old desires and impressions are tied up
And controlled,
The higher mind can be transformed into
Pure illumination.
Then there is contentment!*

*⁓ 37*

Sound arises in
The inner sky of pure consciousness,
The heart-space in the head,
The sky of the heart.
What manifests is Life-Power, the One.
The individual differs from the Universal
As the river differs from the sea.
It is a difference of degree only.

Give up the idea of "I" and "mine"—
It is the cause of continual rebirth.
To think constantly of "I" and "mine"
Is of little intelligence and causes you to take
Lower birth.
The energy of both the sun and the gas lamp
Manifests as light.
Those who have lost the distinction between
Day and night
Find no difference between the light of the sun
And the light of the gas lamp.

Faith is the greatest thing.
In this world nothing is higher!

Black magic and tricks only have effect
If you believe in them.
Concentrate your faith on the breath and
Your thoughts will follow.
Enjoy that which holds your faith!

 38

Rama!
To repeat a name of God brings pure delight—
The bliss of the Self,
True and eternal joy,
Delight in the inner Self,
Kundalini delight.
Rama is the king of mind.
Rama is the essence of the ten senses.
Rama is the Self.
Ravana represents our bad qualities.
Sita is the pure mind.
Lakshmana is persistent concentration.
Krishna is introspection; seeing the Self within.
And seeing the Self within
Is the eternal inner delight.*

39

Mantra is Brahmarandhra,
The prime minister of vital breath—
The spaceless, timeless, causeless point.
In this point is the eternal mantra.
In this point is the sky of consciousness.
This is the supreme joy,
The supreme medicine, the supreme guru,
Whose mantra is: That you are; you are That!*

 40

Behind the many minds is the one pure Mind:
The Mind of All,
The eternal Mind,
Supreme bliss.
The subtle Mind is the sky of the heart—
Pure, unbounded consciousness.

The pure Mind is the pure sky,
True yogic attainment,
Yoga,
Union with God.
This is the heart.

Fulfillment is possible only when you merge
With this pure heart.

There, all idea of "you" and "I" disappears.
In the sky of the heart is liberation, love,
And devotion,
The creative power of the Divine.
Intelligence dwells there.
When you live there, all attachments burn away.
The pure sky is Brahmarandhra.

 41

Pure consciousness is in the upward direction.
What is called male is a subtle state.
What is called female is dynamic.

 42

The search for truth,
Where the subtle merges with the gross,
Requires subtle discrimination.
The seat of such discrimination is in
The sky of the heart.

When the kundalini rises
To this place in the head,
Then the breath is single
And the universe is in one's Self.

All is in the Self—creation, dissolution,
All forms, all events.
And all are seen in the One.
To see separateness is hell;
To see unity is liberation.
Absolute love and devotion are liberation
And complete, endless peace is the goal—
Yogananda, Paramananda, the highest bliss!

The ocean is greater than all the rivers;
It has no limits,
And its water cannot be measured.
It is not possible to cultivate love and
Devotion by giving up the cycle
Of worldly existence.
Instead, remain in the world and attain liberation
By being "this thing" and doing "that thing."

Desire is worldly existence! Samsara!
Desirelessness is liberation!
Eternal bliss, the joy of being and knowledge,
The Self, God, the One—
All are the same.
The highest state is boundless peace.
Liberation is eternal bliss.
Love and devotion are the state of
Being-Consciousness-Bliss!*

 43

Inner initiation is the true fulfillment;
It means "to dwell near"—
The individual merging in the Divine.
Such initiation is internal, subtle.
Subtle discrimination is the third eye
And fulfillment is to be near God.

Initiation is not for the body but beyond—
To the thought of the Self.
One who has performed such discrimination
Is a priest.

Subtle discrimination is the
Sushumna channel in the subtle body.
It is the channel of God,
Where gods and goddesses dwell!

 44

One who has not realized the truth is a beggar.
One who has not destroyed delusion
And left the worldly path is a beggar.

 45

The body is the soul's house.
To distinguish "this house" and "that house"
Takes subtle discrimination.
The house of the gross body is a beggarly house
But who can describe Brahmananda!
Joy of the highest reality!
Truly know that the eternal is One in all.

Hari is not the knower—Shiva is the knower!
Hari is wandering, Hari is demanding:

"Hari, I want this! I want that! Give me!"
This is useless and does not bring happiness.
Let Hari merge in Hara; burn Hari in Hara.
Crying "Hari, Hari" is mental delusion.
Turn away from delusion—turn within!

Shiva is the giver of eternal delight,
The giver of eternal liberty and devotion.
Hari keeps the mind in the world,
Shiva keeps the universe within.
Hari shows the downward path,
Shiva guides us to the path of bliss,
The upward path of liberation.
Hari is like a horse without reins!*

## 46

Fragrances of musk, sandalwood paste,
And camphor
Are experiences of the head.
Where the Om sound is experienced there is
No ignorance.
Ants swarm where there is sugar!

The spiritual eye—not the physical eye—
Sees the real heart.
The head is the highest.
The origin of breath is the bliss
Of one's own Self.
Real bliss is in the cave of the heart.

The house of breath is
The dwelling place of kundalini,
The house of Shiva, the house of fulfillment,
The house of balance and harmony.
One who lives in this house cares not about
Honor or dishonor.

This is the home of the yogi who has
Renounced everything.

This is the home of subtle discrimination,
The home of kundalini,
The home within the heart.

 47

Those whose minds are pure
May call God by any name.
Experience is the train, wisdom is the passenger,
The chakras are the stations.

The subtle is in the chakras.
In the subtle channels is the kundalini shakti—
Together they are Om.
Realize and know the subtle.

# HIGHER MIND

*buddhi*

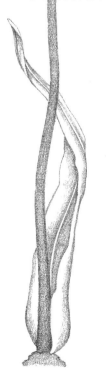

Achutamama was a great devotee from the earliest days in Udipi. He followed Nityananda everywhere. One day in 1920 some local scholars were holding a symposium on metaphysics. One of the pundits had a great intuitive respect for Nityananda and invited him to attend, even though on a strictly scholastic basis he would not have been asked. Nityananda took his faithful but illiterate devotee with him. They both listened to the discussions and eventually Nityananda was asked to say a few words. He immediately turned to his unfortunate companion and prodded him to rise and speak. Achutamama was totally taken aback and even a little angry, thinking how unfair it was of the Master to play such a cruel joke on him. But the prodding went on and finally he had no choice but to rise. At once he found words flowing from him. He never knew what he said but it must have been acceptable because he finished to smiles and applause from the assembly!

In 1916, as some villagers crossed the railroad tracks north of Pandalaquin Railway Station, one man had a seizure. He fell on the tracks, frothing from his mouth, and a helpless crowd soon gathered. Suddenly, a thin dark-skinned young man appeared in their midst, smiling calmly. He put some ash miraculously manifested in the dying man's mouth—

and instantly it was as if nothing had ever happened to him. (See the glossary entry for *vibhuti*.) The man stood up completely cured and the dark young man, ignoring the growing crowd, simply sat down on the tracks. As the excited crowd continued to grow, someone called out that he was none other than Ishwar Iyer's Nityananda.

Soon the railroad authorities appeared, annoyed by the large crowd near the tracks. Now, the local sub-inspector had such a reputation for terrorizing the poor railway coolies that he was nicknamed "Kaduva" ("Tiger"). This man had taken up the unfortunately common English attitude of looking contemptuously at native Indian culture and spirituality. Therefore when he saw the large crowd gathered around the silent, dark young man, he stormed into the crowd and shouted abuse at Nityananda, threatening to kill him if he came near the station. But Nityananda simply smiled and moved a little further down the tracks as if he had not heard Kaduva at all.

Soon it was time for the Madras/Mangalore Express to arrive. Kaduva directed the Anglo-Indian driver to continue at full speed, crushing the mad man if he would not listen. But to every one's great surprise, Nityananda burst into gales of laughter and the massive engine came to a grinding halt. All the efforts of the engineer notwithstanding, the train would not budge a single inch.

Like a huge tree felled, Kaduva fell at the feet of the smiling Nityananda and begged his pardon. Demonstrating his major change of heart, the railway man constructed a small ashram for Bhagavan at the village of Kothamangalam. Nityananda stayed there for three days and then left.

48

In the Indivisible,
There is no divisible.

For one who has realized the Self,
There is no ignorance.

For the ignorant,
There is no wisdom.

A mother loves all her children equally.
Even if they trouble and beat her,
She does not cast them out.

One who is Self-realized loves all equally.

49

A person who knows the Self has no mind—
Seeing all things equally;
Being beyond the three states of
Sleep, dream, and deep sleep;
Experiencing neither sunrise nor sunset.

The soot-covered glass chimney of a lamp
Reflects light poorly and
Must be kept clean.
Likewise, removing the soot of ignorance
From the mind allows it to clearly reflect
The light of the Self within.*

50

A true spiritual person
Renounces worldly pleasures
And by practicing yoga
Experiences complete union with
The divine force within.
Bliss can only be experienced—
It does not come from listening.

One who has experienced divine bliss
Is a realized soul,
A mahatma.
This does not happen by
Seeing stone and earth—
It only happens by seeing the Self within.

 51

The essential knowledge must be attained
By everyone.
And what is this essential knowledge?
For the individual Self to know
The mystery of the universal Self!

52

The true goal of human life is wisdom.
One who does not know this is just an animal.
One who does not know this is not a true person.

Human life is the highest in Creation.
Do not spend it like a frog in the water,
Rising and sinking, rising and sinking,
Again and again.

Human life is the highest in creation;
It cannot always be attained.
When the opportunity is there,
Work toward the goal.

First cook, then eat:
Discrimination is the fire,
Intelligence the vessel,
Liberation the goal.

_53_

The head is the ocean of delight,
The seat of bliss,
The thousand-petalled lotus,
The seat of liberation.
Knowledge of this is not found in books—
It is inherent in the brain!

Books are made up of parts
But the knowledge that shines in the head is
One undivided whole.
A book has many chapters,
But this knowledge has only one.
Books are for those not established
In this knowledge.
For the person with realization,
Knowledge is stable, eternal, and indivisible.

A person is born with a brain—not a book!
At the moment of death, there is no book.
Only in between do you take up a book.*

54

No one criticizes the king to his face—
Only behind his back.
Likewise, worldly people dare not
Criticize spiritual knowledge directly.

Entering a dark room after being in the
Bright sun, you see nothing.
Emerging from the dark into the light,
You cannot know from whence you have come.

 55

Birds are like airplanes.
Animals are like people.
People are like animals.

A person graced with spiritual knowledge is
Like a dog.

Feed it once and it will remember until it dies.
It will have constant love for the master
Who fed it only once.

Most people have no subtle discrimination;
They never know where they are going.
But one with perfect understanding
Has constant love and devotion.

 56

The gross state is of the mind.
The subtle state is of the Self.
People with spiritual knowledge are always in
The yogic sleep of awareness.

Whether walking or sitting,
They are like the tortoise
Projecting arms and legs
Only when they are needed.
At other times,
He withdraws them into the shell.

57

Those with minds merged in samadhi are
Not deluded by the external magic show.
They fear nothing;
To them, there is no fear in the world.

In their presence, the tiger and the cobra
Forget their aggressiveness.
All creatures become calm.
Enemies forget their hostility and become quiet.

Why?
Because of the doubt.
There is no darkness then—
The mind is purified by pure light, happiness,
And harmony.

58

Just as a woman carrying a burden on her head
Concentrates on balance,
Just as the actor playing the king
Concentrates on the crown,
So the attention of one with spiritual knowledge
Concentrates on the steady mind.

59

Fill the lamp with oil and light the wick.
As the oil burns and the wick shortens,
The light dims.
But if the oil is replenished and the wick is set,
The lamp will shine as before.

The inner life of a spiritual person is similar.
Like butter mixed with water,
The butter does not sink to the bottom
But rises to the top!

Body is the water, spirit is the butter.
Subtle intelligence should be in the head;
The higher mind should be at the top

Of the sushumna channel
Wherein flows kundalini's life-force.

Both mind and higher mind should reside
In the head:
Mind in the head, mind in the higher mind,
Wisdom in the mind.
A steady mind brings discrimination and thereby
The union of the individual with the Self.

 60

A house without lamplight offers
Neither hospitality nor warmth.
In such a house, people bump into each other
And the furniture.

In your house, let the lamp be wisdom!
Let the light be kundalini!

61

With mind, you want everything.
With no mind, you want nothing.
With mind, you see "god" as a separate being.
When mind merges with the higher mind,
No separate god is needed.
All is seen as One.

Desires require a god to fulfill them.
Your mind chases the objects of the senses
And doubt arises,
Leading to a need for an image to worship.
Cause and effect appear separate—
This is delusion and ignorance!

 62

Once you learn to write on paper,
There is no need to write in sand spread on the floor.
Once you attain knowledge of the state of
The Absolute
Without name, form, or attributes,
There is no need to study its many forms.
Can curds be changed back into milk?

Until his brain develops,
A baby sees no differences in the world
Around him.
A rock and a diamond are the same to him—
Something to grasp and toss away.

A true yogi is like this.
A lump of dirt and money are the same
To one who has realized the Self.
Such a person is not attached to either one,
Seeing all as the Self—
The Self in all and all in the Self.

This is inner vision, subtle thought;
This is Shiva-Shakti,
The creative power of the indivisible One.
And God's creative power is the Self,
The One reality.

64

Where water flows
There is no mud.

Ignorance is the mud and
Devotion and wisdom are the water.

 65

When a speck of dust blows into your eye,
Your full attention turns to it.
Attention turned inward—
This is inner sight!

Ignorance is like a box filled with dust.
Only the person who filled the box
Knows its contents.
No one else knows.

The power and energy of life are the real wealth.
A steady mind is the box.
Place the wealth in the box and lock it.
Now the mind is in its proper place in the head.

Our duty is to return the treasure given to us—
The treasure of the Self.
Return to the Self within and
Know your own secret!

The universe is inside you and
You are inside the universe.
The inner Self is the One dancing in all—
The One who is here and the One who is there.

Again, know your own secret!

66

The supreme light is also the universal light.
O mind, discard the idea of "otherness" and
Hold onto the "sameness"!

All seeds have the same power inside.
Subtlety in all seeds is One —
Differences are in behavior only.

The mind's delusions are not permanent.
Everything seen and heard
Is temporary.

You were born with breath,
And when you depart,
You leave only breath.

This body of earth is not made
Or taken away.
The gift of Shiva is the same for all!

Freedom from doubt is the path to
One-pointedness of mind.
The intelligence of doubters dwindles
Because wherever they look,
They see only doubt. After all,
We are each subject to our own nature;
There is no reason to find qualities
Not there!

Just as you cannot see your reflection in
Agitated water,
Fickle-minded people cannot see their
Real nature.
Those with steady minds, however,
See the One, the Indivisible,
Everywhere they look.
They see themselves in others.

Through red glasses,
Things appear red—not green!
We each see according to our thinking.

68

Only when the well is emptied
And cleansed of accumulated mud
Can the pure water of the spring flow freely.

Divine wisdom is like the flowing spring water—
Burn away the accumulated thought
Of "I" and "mine"
And allow true knowledge to pour forth
In its simple purity.

 69

In deep sleep, there is no mind.
In deep sleep, you are near the Self.
In the states of waking, dreaming,
And thought-play,
You are deceived into a sense of active participation.
Remember that this is not real!

Merge the knowledge of the Unseen with the Seen
And find perfect bliss.
Only one who has attained such knowledge is a
Swami, Yogi, and Guru!

70

When the life-force moves
In an outward direction,
Desires are born.
There the mind follows, dividing and subdividing
Into the two-, four-, and six-fold properties of
Unconscious cosmic Nature and
What we call "the world" comes into being.

All other worldly attributes arise from
This beginning.
Once born, a person most needs
The organs of knowledge.
The five organs of action relate to the earth.
The five organs of knowledge relate to the
Gross consciousness.

Those who conquer the senses are free!
For them, fulfillment arises from within.

71

Mind is the root of bondage and liberation,
Of good and evil,
Of sin and holiness.

Mind creates thought,
Thought leads to action,
And  action leads to results.

Without mind, there is no speech—
No coming and no going,
Nothing happens!

In school, it is not enough to speak English.
You must learn to write it.
Only then can you pass to the next grade

## 72

Thinking and reflecting is what makes a person.
A true person thinks and reflects.
Ignorance of the path to the Self leads to rebirth
Again and again.

Without knowledge of this path,
You will not find contentment.
Contentment comes from knowing
The path of spirituality.
It comes from doing your work without
Being attached to its results.
This is desirelessness, liberation, divine bliss.

Desire is hell!
Desirelessness is supreme joy!
The highest state is Shiva-Shakti—
The experience of the Here and the Beyond.

73

At the beginning,
Mind and Self are the same.

At the end,
In the state of universal dissolution,
They are also the same.

Only in the interval
Of breathing, thinking, and actions
Are they different.

 74

Perfect concentration is the means by which
The higher mind increases its power
Of understanding.
It is a path to liberation,
A path to the highest.

Perfect concentration is a means to steady the
Breath of Life—
For when it is steady, the mind becomes steady.
When the vital breath turns upward,
Divine wisdom enters every nerve and
Peace is the result.

Then, nature and the subtle are separate.
Then, the higher mind can experience yoga-power,
Peace, forgiveness, and contentment.
By practicing perfect concentration,
You find the whole world within.
The mind so steadied enjoys eternal bliss!

The Self is beyond all karma.
True karma is work done
Without attachment to its fruits.
True karma is work done in the
Knowledge of the Self,
Actionless and passionless.
There is no sin without the sense of doing.

75

As a lamp cannot burn without oil,
So the body cannot function without breath.
Without a rudder, a boat cannot be steered
To harbor.
A steamship is guided by steam power and
The captain's skill.
A rowboat cannot forge ahead like the steamship.
One who resides in the world is like the rowboat.

One devoted to the spiritual path
Who has brought the world inside
Is like the steamship.
For such a person the Brahmarandhra is
Like the guiding light atop the steamship.
The mind is merged in the sky of the heart,
The chakra at the top of the head
Where kundalini is one with the Self.
The light is the spiritual seeker.

The cow cannot run like the horse.
One whose mind is merged in the Self is
Like the horse.

One whose mind resides in the world is
Like the cow.
Not everyone can be king at the same time.
Nor can everyone be shopkeepers.
Someone must be a subject!
Someone must be a customer!

 76

The seeds of the mind
When fed into the mill of
Spiritual discernment
Produce the oil of "wisdom-nectar."

 77

Without faith there can be no desirelessness.
When the mind is dissolved there can be no desire.
Without faith there can be no fruits.

Only the mind's delusion pays a fortune
For diamonds.
Without the mind, diamonds are just
Lumps of earth.

78

The selfish mind is neither firm nor steady.
Only subtle discrimination is
Steady.

Creation is peace, creation is the Witness,
Creation is subtle discrimination.
This discrimination gives nourishment
And liberation.

Cleverness is not superior to
The creative power of the Divine.
Rather, this power contains cleverness.
Cleverness is a modification of the mind.

Real intelligence is subtle discrimination.
True power is subtle discrimination—
The higher mind.

 79

No one is mad in this world!*

80

A person without desire has no need of
A separate god,
No need to strive for anything.
When the mind chases desires,
One must strive to attain one-pointedness.

Concentrate the mind in the higher mind
As long as the pulse beats,
As often as the pulse beats.
Do not unite the mind with the senses.
Whatever you do, keep the inner state aloof!

As a person sinking under water must learn
To swim,
Conquer Maya's delusions with conscious effort.
It is delusion that causes you to experience
Different states
As your mind runs into various objects.

You cling to the coconut tree—
The coconut tree does not cling to you.
After all, does Maya have arms and legs
To seize you?

81

As camphor is consumed in fire,
So the mind must be consumed in the Self.

The moment camphor catches fire,
It is transformed
And burns itself out of existence, leaving no trace.

When mind merges in the Self,
No trace of ego remains.

 82

As water is contained in a reservoir,
So must the mind be contained and
Not run uncontrolled like a
Monsoon-swollen river.

Mind is the cause of good and evil.
God does neither good nor evil—
They are ideas of the mind.

Knowledge and wisdom come from the Divine;
Accept the protection of its supreme armor—
Not even bullets can pierce it!

83

The umbrella does not hold you—
All is held by the mind.
When the mind's moods are conquered,
All difference disappears.

Those devoted to the spiritual life are
Without desire; they are true yogis.
A person with mind wants everything,
One with no mind possesses everything inside.

Just as a steamship carries all things needed
For the journey,
So those who overcome the mind
Carry the universe within.

84

Subtle intellect is the spiritual wisdom of the
Higher mind.
Inner concentration is one-pointed.
Gross intellect is like a horse unreined—
Neither steady nor permanent,
Neither Hari nor Shiva.

Knowledge from the guru is
Subtle intelligence—not gross!
Gross intelligence is the intelligence of animals.
He is not a man who does not return
What he has been given.
She is not a woman who does not return
what she has been given.

85

It is the mind that observes the vow of silence—
Not the tongue.
Whatever is done when intelligence and wisdom
Are united in the Self is not karma.
Silence is native to the mind—
Not the tongue.
Spiritual practice, the pursuit of an ideal,
Is achieved through silence.

A yogi unites intelligence and wisdom,
Placing the mind in and under the control of
The higher mind.
The three primary channels through which
Conscious creative energy circulates
In the subtle body are
The ida, the pingala, and the sushumna.
Sushumna is the seat of kundalini.
The discipline of silence is really the
Brahmarandhra,
The sahasrara chakra at the top of the head,
The junction of the three channels.*

86

One who renounces all sense of
Honor or dishonor
Is filled with true bliss,
Brahmananda,
Union with the Absolute.
Concentrate the workings of the mind
And intellect for even five minutes and
Everything becomes That.

Those who do not recognize the universal Cause
Do not understand the purpose of life.
Like moths attracted to the fatal flame,
They are caught in Maya's net of delusion.
Like moths, they live in view of the flame,
Playing in and around it,
Only to fall in at last and perish.

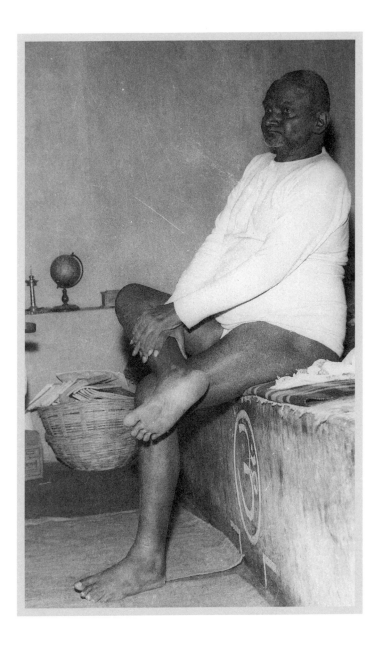

# THE POWER OF OM

*omkar*

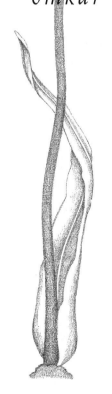

Nityananda was always totally immersed in the Divine, in Omkar, in the power and the sound of Om. Achutamama, a devotee from the South Kanara years, recalls the following incident: Near the coastal village of Kaup there was a lighthouse; it was under the charge of an English caretaker who admired Nityananda and made him welcome whenever he wished to come. One night, Nityananda took Achutamama to the top of the lighthouse. Pointing out a large ship lying at anchor in the distance, Nityananda asked his companion to estimate the depth of the sea at the ship. To the answer, "It must be quite deep for a ship like that," the youthful Nityananda replied, "Oh no! It is only ankle deep. Come, I will show you."

It was a dark night. As soon as they got into the sea, Nityananda took his devotee's arm with his right hand and stretched his left hand out in front of them. They walked in ankle-deep water all the way to the side of the ship. The bewildered Achutamama did not understand and could not answer when Nityananda told him, "See, it is only ankle-deep as you were told." They turned around and walked back as they had come, Nityananda again holding his companion with one hand while he held the other arm stretched out. Halfway to shore, Nityananda lowered his outstretched hand; both men immediately sank into the deep sea. Achutamama was terrified, but in seconds Nityananda reached him and pulled him up. Again they started walking through ankle-deep water, with Nityananda's left hand out-stretched as before. Upon returning to the room where they were to spend the night, the exhausted Achutamama immediately fell into a deep sleep. He awoke at about midnight. Nityananda was sitting up looking at him. Seeing that his companion was awake, Nityananda began to speak. He said that what had happened was a manifestation of the Omkar Shakti and that everything in the universe was a manifestation of this Omkar. As soon as he had heard these two sentences, Achutamama fell back into his deep sleep.

Whenever devotees would begin to tell their tales of woe, Nityananda would wave them aside, saying: "Everything is known. Did the Pandavas moan to Krishna about their difficulties? Was he not aware of them?"

A young wife in Mangalore was often reprimanded by her husband for her devotion to Nityananda and for visiting places where he was found. Once in a rage over her disobedience, he lashed her with a belt until blood was drawn. Days later, the devotee had a chance to see Nityananda and immediately told him of her plight. The Master replied, "You got the lash but who got the pain? See?" And he turned to show her his back with marks of the lashing.

Another woman, pure, simple, and very devout, visited Nityananda in the mid-fifties and recounted some worries of her own. Nityananda shook his head: "Have you not yet understood who this one is? Are you not convinced of this place? Still worrying? Have faith and conviction. Everything will happen in its time."

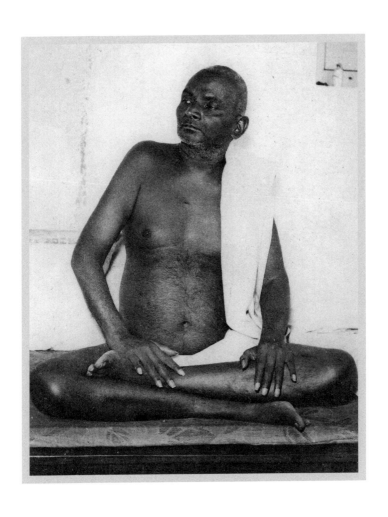

87

Omkar!
The power of Om is One.
It is the universal force.
In Om is creation
And the dissolution of creation.
In Om is the dissolution of the mind.

Atman!
The power of Om is the eternal Self within you.
Om is indivisible—
Anything that can be divided is not the whole!
From the beginning, God reveals only one truth.

Seated inside a closed room,
One is unaware of anything "outside."
With the door shut,
The embodied Self and the Supreme Self are one.
When the door opens,
The mind separates the two
And they appear distinct.

88

All is He,
The One pervading all,
The One beyond all qualities.
He is One, He is Om!

His form is everlasting peace.
He blesses those who trust in Him
And punishes those who ridicule.
He eases the time of death for devotees.

O God! Turn me
From the downward path
And show me the middle way.
The giver is Shiva.

89

All things are forms of Om's power.
Omkar is the divine in them,
Omkar is the subtle pause preceding creation.

As the vital breath,
Omkar pervades all things,
Inner and outer.

It is impossible to describe pure consciousness
And the creative power of the Divine
Unless you have experienced them.

It is impossible to describe the Self
Unless you have experienced it.
Book knowledge is useless!

90

God manifests in the form of peace.
Om is the form of peace.
He is without form,
Without change.
He is above discrimination,
Absolute.

Like a baby rocked to sleep in a cradle,
With the mind as the pillow,
Sleep inwardly.

 91

The Self resides in the cave of the body.
Freedom from the bondage of duality is the
Highest goal.
The physical body has many different parts
But the power that creates and sustains it is
One and indivisible.

The power of Om pervades the entire universe,
Its resonance pervades the form.
Om has neither form nor shape.

92

Does the sound arise from the universe
Or does the universe arise from the sound?
Does effect follow cause
Or does cause follow effect?

The universe arises from sound.
As do all things with form,
From sound, form arises.
From the cause is the effect.
But how does the cause arise?

Both cause and effect are to serve one's Self.
Both cause and effect arise from the Self.
In the Self, cause and effect merge into One.
The delusion that arises in the Self
Subsides into the Self.

A lie is a lie.
If you believe a lie, then you must speak the lie.
If you believe the truth, then you must speak
The truth.

Those who speak falsely have no truth in them,
No falsehood separate from them.
Falsehood is one with them.

What is the cause of falsehood?
People become so accustomed to it
That it no longer looks false.
They are unaware of any separate thing
Called "falsehood."
If they do recognize falsehood as separate,
Then they will no longer incline to it.
They will look for the good
And find the right path!

## 93

The subtle state,
The omnipresent universal force,
Is the same in everything and everywhere.
There is no distinction between the moving
And the still.
There is difference only in causation.

Difference is delusion!
Difference is in the body, and the body
Is transient.
To see the subtle in the gross is liberation.
Liberation is indivisible.
Liberation is in the sky of the heart!

In the heart is the Shiva linga,
The subtle space containing the whole universe
In the process of formation and dissolution.
In the heart is self-existence,
Vital air, the upward breath, the breath of life.

The universal life-force is the One in all.
To those who practice and see, it is the One.
To those who do not practice, there is only
The bondage of desire.
Withdraw the desires and attain
Liberation in this life!
Realize the One principle,
Turn the eye inward and see the truth.

One who has turned the mind inward is
A pure conscious being;
The universe is in him and he is in the universe.
The mind, when involved in the world,
Cannot be steady.
The Absolute, pure consciousenss,
Shiva in the heart—
They are steady, they are One,
They are the power of Om.

The power of Om united with forms is the
Universal sound.
The power of Om is "disassociation" of
Bodily awareness.

## 94

The power of Om is all-pervading.
Like the rising of the sun,
It is the witness of all things.
The power of Om is the most frightful
Of all forms for it is fire.
And nothing is greater than fire!
All is fire—
Within and without.

Earth is in the middle, above is air.
Air is in the universe, the universe is in the air.
Air is first, fire is second.
Thought is first, sound is second.
Soundlessness is in the form of air.
Soundlessness is eternal delight.
It is the bliss of being and consciousness.
Merge your Self in soundlessness!

All the visible universe is in the Self.
When consciousness and being are merged,
There is bliss, joy, delight!

Joy of discrimination! Vivekananda!
Joy of consciousness! Chaitanyananda!
Joy of Brahman! Brahmananda!
Joy of the Supreme! Paramananda!
Eternal joy! Nityananda!
Joy of being and consciousness!
Satchitananda!

This is true adulthood.
This is wisdom—
The wisdom of God,
The wisdom of yoga,
The wisdom of time.
Find "Three time wisdom" in the heart.
Liberation and eternal bliss are in the heart!

## 95

Om vibrates like a storm in the sky.
Having neither beginning nor end,
It is the stage manager of the Divine Drama.

The human body is a string of Om,
All that is—inside us, outside us,
Is born of Om.

We do not need to search for Om.
It is present in everything, everywhere.
No special effort is needed to recall it
To memory.

Shakti! The creative power of the Divine
That is Om exists in all creatures.
The sound produced by any creature is
Nothing but Om.

The universal sound is Om.
When Om unites with vital breath
And moves in the body,
This is the universal sound.
When nature and the subtle energy are separate,

This is the universal sound;
When both are felt to be one,
This is the Oneness.

Om is seen everywhere.
Wherever you place your faith
Becomes All.

The Shakti that is Om
Fills and penetrates the universe.
It is formless, infinite, and indivisible.
It is the light in all directions!

Ignorance and knowledge are not real—
Neither pain nor pleasure has effect.
All is Om!

## 96

The energy of Om is like an infinite ocean
Moving in all directions.
It pervades all, both inside and outside.
In the form of the higher mind,
It becomes creation, preservation,
And dissolution—
It becomes soundless.
The unstruck sound merges in the higher mind.
The higher mind dissolves in the Om sound.

All merge and become one:
Om and reason,
The world and the higher mind.
The world and Om merge into the sky of
The heart…
The sky of the heart merges into the
Higher mind…
The higher mind merges into consciousness…
Consciousness and the higher mind merge
Into the power of Om…
Wisdom and the imperishable merge into the
Higher mind…

The higher mind merges into the Self
And the Self into the higher mind...
All thoughts of Form into Self merge
Through the higher mind...
Cause and effect merge into Self...
Knowledge and ignorance become one with
The Self
Through the path of the higher mind.

Peace is as pure as the sky of consciousness!
A deep purity beyond the distinctions of
Pure and impure;
Eternally pure,
Formless and changeless.
In peace, form and change unite with the
Higher mind,
Expanding infinitely in all directions through
All things,
Eternally equal.
Peace has no purpose, no motive;
Never associate peace with motive—
For it is quite separate!
It is the highest state.

By the path of the higher mind,

Peace is neither of this world nor of the next.

It is not touched by pleasure or pain.

Understanding that there is one Self in all—

This is true peace!

Such peace gives happiness both Here and There.

This is the word of Veda, the holy law, liberation—

The fulfillment of human birth.

It is Truth, it is the highest state, it is All.

It is desireless devotion, an absence of desire,

Freedom from cares.

This is the true state of the Self!

O mind!

Surrender your desire for this thing and that thing!

Serve the Self, serve the Truth.

Delight in the Self's inner plan.

Delight in the bliss of consciousness and being.

Forget day and night and dwell forever

In the light of the higher mind.

See the entire universe as nothing but the Self.

Let the Self encompass the three states of

Waking, sleep, and deep sleep.
Cultivate the great peace in the Self.
Sing its glory to all the universe!

The mind will understand Truth through
The intellect.
Truth is not a religion—it cannot be taught.
You must first discover Truth in your own Self
And then let it expand in Om.
Sacrifice memory to the higher mind.
Quiet your consciousness
And let Truth alone remain.
Merge Truth in the sky of the heart.
Be one with the sky of consciousness!
See the universe with equal vision
And dissolve the sense of "you" and "I."
Recognize Truth with this same-sightedness.
There is nothing other than Truth!
This is the state of Satchitananda.
Truth is the beginning and Truth is the end.
Truth is inside and and Truth is outside.
Truth is One.

Through concentration and understanding
Establish this Truth of oneness in your heart—
This is the highest state.
Truth is the juice of the fruit that grows
On the tree of desirelessness,
The sweet juice of wisdom, the sweet juice of yoga,
That transforms every quality of the body.
Direct it upward and shake off all doubts
By bathing in the waters of Shiva!
Let Shiva and Shakti unite with Om.

See the forms and properties of the world
With the third eye.
Burn all doubts—the six enemies—to ashes:
Anger, desire, envy, passion, greed, delusion.
Cover yourself with these ashes and join Shiva.
Enter the third eye:
You are Shiva and Shiva is you!
Do not hesitate to sacrifice the difference
Between you and Shiva—
Throw it into the fire of the five senses!
Sacrifice all doubts and all qualities in these fires.

Established in desirelessness,
Drink the nectar every moment
And drink freely!

Knowing Truth, there is no fear of death.
Knowing Truth, death is just
An external condition—
Like sleep.
"I" and "mine" are an obstruction
On the path to God;
They are a fear of death.
Truth holds no distinction between
Inner and outer;
With the senses turned inward,
"I" and "mine" dwindle to nothing.
Only when awakening from sleep and
Becoming aware of the external
Do you understand the nature of sleep.
Wisdom, too, is like this!

Control your desires!
Birth and death are caused by desire:
Desire transforms shadows into reality.

In the discriminating higher mind,
The fear of birth and death disappears.
When the mind is subject to desire,
You experience pleasure and pain—
You need external help.
But with desire controlled,
Pleasure and pain have no influence.
Become the slave to your habits and
You will take a lower birth.
Control your habits! Exercise your will!
Work done on a whim is temporary—
But work done by exercising the higher mind
Has life-long benefit!

Whims and fancies are never permanent—
They are as inferior to the higher mind
As the little finger is to the middle finger.
Strong attachments to particular things
Create tendencies carried along
From life to life.
Such tendencies are the cause of rebirth.
Tendencies regarding the physical body
Come and go

Like bubbles in water—
But strong attachments create tendencies
That cause another birth!
Their special form reflects one's internal state.
For a person with a strong tendency,
Whatever work is done involves
Only the body—not the Self.
This is because the tendency of such a person
Stands apart, breathing the body.
And when the body cannot satisfy the tendency,
It is discarded and a new body is found.
Hence, another birth—
A birth solely for the fulfillment of
That strong tendency.

Think!
Is it possible to raise both feet at once
While walking?
One foot must be put down
Before the other is lifted.
So it is with the tendencies of former birth.

# SPIRITUAL PRACTICE

*sadhana*

Lakshmansa Khoday was a very great devotee. Just twelve hours before Nityananda's *mahasamadhi* he arrived at Ganeshpuri to receive darshan of the Bhagavan. Seeing the weakened condition of his guru's body, Lakshmansa was moved to tears, and when, even in this condition, the lover of devotees ordered coffee for him, he could bear it no longer. He begged Nityananda to use his Shakti to cure himself. But Nityananda, the incarnation of love and kindness, said, "Shakti is not for this body—it is for the devotees."

As is the custom with many Hindus, the narrator of this incident invited the thin, dark sadhu home to stay for the night, as he was impressed by the bearing of the young man. Given a room, the sadhu asked him for a string. Wondering at this strange request, the host decided to sleep in the same room. When he returned, he was surprised to see the young man carefully attaching the string to swing between two walls. The host was even more surprised a few minutes later, when the young sadhu climbed up on the string, stretched out, and went to sleep. He was apparently totally comfortable, as he turned this way and that, a picture of complete rest and tranquillity.

Remembering similar incidents in the life of Sai Baba of Shirdi, the devotee lay there, lost in the sheer wonder of it. In the morning, the young sadhu awoke and, remarking that it was time for the train to Kanhangad to come, went out. Only when the train could be heard leaving the station nearby could the host arise. And only then did he realize that he had been with the great saint of Kanhangad, Nityananda.

On hearing of Swamiji, fishermen from the coastal area of Kanhangad started flocking to him; their leader's name was Poklon. After he saw devotees bring vegetarian dishes for Nityananda, Poklon brought some cooked rice and curry made of crabs. With great devotion and simplicity, he fed Nityananda the food he had brought; the Bhagavan ate it all and smiled. That night Poklon and his son went out with their fishing nets, only to run into a sudden, savage storm with heavy rain, thunder, and high winds. As the boat capsized, both father and son were knocked unconscious. They recovered to realize that their boat was righted and they were being towed to shore by an unknown boatman. As their eyes cleared, the men were filled with wonder: the boatman was none other than Nityananda and in their unharmed boat were their nets filled with fish.

A devotee recalls his first chance meeting with Nityananda in Kanhangad. It was 1929; the devotee was traveling with his family to another ashram near Kanhangad, but the railroad porter on hearing of their destination urged them to see Nityananda as well. The porter was very enthusiastic; he said that while Nityananda did not have an official ashram, he was a truly extraordinary saint who was very kind to the poor and lowly no matter what their faith. Interested, they proceeded to the old fort area where the rock temple was erected in 1963. There was an entrance in the broken wall of the old fort, and the party was told that Nityananda often used this dilapidated gateway.

After a long wait, Nityananda appeared and entered the old gate, walking briskly. The family hurried after him, but he had disappeared completely and so they returned to the entrance. It was early spring and the mangoes were still ripening on the trees. Some local boys began to throw stones at the tender young fruit when Nityananda reappeared and he called to the boys to stop. They immediately changed their target and began hurling stones at the Bhagavan. But before anyone could react, a strange sight met their eyes: each stone that touched Nityananda fell down as a sweet.

More stones were thrown and more sweets fell. Without a word, Nityananda walked away and disappeared again into the jungle. The boys were busy collecting sweets. The devotee and his family resumed their journey to the other ashram. They had seen how a saint behaves: giving sweets for stones.

Kanaran, a successful Bombay hotelier and a loyal devotee, went to Ganeshpuri every Thursday for darshan of Nityananda. In spite of this, he found it impossible to obey when he was ordered to close down his flourishing hotel. (Nityananda's actual words were: "Hotel bandh."). There soon followed calamity after calamity; in an astonishingly short time, Kanaran was reduced to begging for food and shelter from friends. He was deeply ashamed, feeling that his affairs were a shambles and his life a failure. Resolving to put an end to his suffering, he went to the sea shore. He waited until after dusk, when the crowds had cleared. Then, in a final gesture of despair, he threw his useless ring of keys far out into the sea, knowing he himself would soon follow. But before he could move, he heard someone calling his name. Turning, Kanaran recognized a close friend, a man from Gujarat. This friend knew Kanaran's history and of his despair; he managed to dissuade him from his plan and took him to a hotel. Incredibly, he produced Kanaran's ring of keys, which should have been deep in the sand of the ocean! Along with the keys, the friend gave the former hotelier some money, then ordered two dinners. Telling the still gaping Kanaran to eat both servings if he did not return soon, the rescuer left. Mysteriously, he did not return and could not be found again.

Times changed and Kanaran again found himself in the long line of devotees waiting for the darshan of Nityananda. When his turn came, Nityananda spoke: "Where is your Gujarat friend?" The smile that accompanied this question revealed the mystery to Kanaran, as he recognized his long-lost "friend." Nityananda then told him how difficult it would have been for him to regain human birth if he had had his way. Reaffirming the necessity of making the best use of the life allotted to him, Kanaran flourished again with Nityananda's blessing.

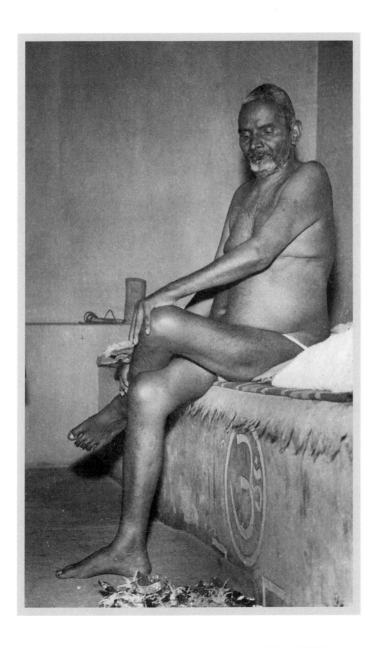

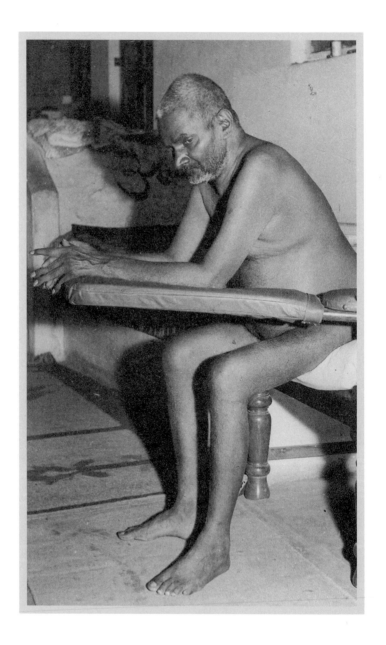

97

Without yoga
There is no escape
From the law of karma.

 98

Only in the subtle state
Can you be without thought.
Discrimination is the merging of mind
Into the higher mind.

Samadhi is the equal vision:
Seeing One in all,
When the fluctuations of the mind
Are stilled.

Through spiritual practice,
Keep the six enemies of

Anger, desire, envy, passion, greed, delusion
Under control.

When you practice,
Do not speak ill of others.
Doing so is like putting a stone
On a young sprouting plant.

Do not relax your practice
Even for fifteen minutes!
The mind should be ceaselessly
In the center.

 99

Act according to your word.
Speak as you intend to act.

 100

Even if you perform purification
For a thousand years,
If you work for results
Self-realization will not come.

Perform purification for even a little while
Without desire, and
You will see God in all
And all in God.

 101

Even a child of five knows there is a God,
But not where He is.

The sun has been the silent witness
Of all time and all events,
Yet how many truly see the sun?

How many people sincerely seek God?
Three-quarters are addicted to the senses;
Less than a quarter even reach the middle state.
A few do good deeds—but many do evil.

102

A true guru can turn you
From the jungle road of ignorance
To the royal road of spiritual knowledge.
There are two gurus:
The causal guru and the action guru.
The guru who gives the disciple a mantra
Or otherwise initiates him into spiritual practice
Is the causal guru.
The Self is the action guru.

No person can be another's action guru—
Only another's causal guru.
The causal guru can lead the thirsty disciple
To the well,
But only one's inner action guru can
Prompt one to drink deeply.
The first instructs, the second acts.
The divine force within all creatures is the Self.
This is the action guru, the supreme guru,
The all-pervading guru—
God.*

103

One does not become a guru by wearing
Orange robes and wooden sandals
Or by using prayer beads.
Preaching the highest truth
But giving the disciples only stones
Is not the behavior of a guru!

People often think the physical teacher is
The guru.
The true guru lives by his teaching
Before teaching others.
He must complete his own spiritual practices
And attain Self-realization
Before he can prove the Truth!

— 104

To ride a horse safely in a crowd
Of two thousand people requires
A capable rider.
Intelligence is above,
Mind is below.

Intelligence is king,
Mind is the minister;
Mind must be subordinate to intelligence.
The first is sound,
The second is the impression that follows.

The primary guru is the Self;
The secondary guru is the one who initiates.
To do and to teach is the role
Of the secondary guru;
To realize is the role of the primary guru.

There is no guru without aspiration.
When you have aspiration,
You require the secondary guru.
The secondary guru leads you to the well—
The primary guru drinks from it.

105

He turns darkness into light,

Ignorance into knowledge.

He reveals the subtle sight in place of the gross.

He is the one guru,

The guru who is in all,

The guru of the universe!

No person can be your guru—

A person can only be secondary.

The real guru is Guru of the Universe:

Om, Brahma, Vishnu,

The Highest, the Absolute,

Origin of All;

Higher than mental modifications,

Higher than the transient Maya

Adorning the body.

Like separating the dried coconut

From the shell,

Give up the body-idea.

This is the highest!

106

Fire has spread itself everywhere!
This highest of all is essential to all creation.
First realize yourself, then impart it to others—
This is the highest duty.
When you are hungry,
Realize that others also feel hunger.
When you are in pain,
Realize that others also feel pain.
Your goal is also the goal of others.

If a doctor knows a remedy
But does not reveal it,
With his death, it is lost to us.
One who does not know the way
To Self-realization is not a true human being.
Of all ways of knowledge,
Self-realization is the highest.
Make this known to all people!
Those who are hungry must be fed!
No one seeks knowledge of the One
Without discriminative power.

107

One who has dissolved the mind
Is the universal teacher.
Such a person has uprooted all desire—
And burnt it to ashes.
For such a person,
The universe is within.

The spiritual path is the heart-space,
The sky of the heart,
Light, pure consciousness, divine light, fire,
Fire with form, internal fire,
The fire of discrimination.

The fire of discrimination is in the universe.

108

Only one who has abandoned all desire is
A spiritual teacher.
He alone is an avadhut,
The highest of men—exalted!

To such a person, this world and the next are one.
He dwells in the sky of consciousness,
The true sky, the sky of liberation in life.

Joy, delight, bliss!
Of self-mastery, of God, of the Real,
Of release from all bonds, of human fulfillment.

The avadhut is the lord of liberation,
The king of understanding!

 109

Avadhuts know that birth and death
Are illusions of the body.
They are no more identified with the body
Than ordinary people are identified

With their garments.
They have gone beyond all qualities:
Shining with the full glow of Self-realization,
At once the light and all that is illuminated,
Fully aware.
Raja yogis—not hatha yogis!

Avadhuts have no sense of "I".
They see everything as projections of the Self,
Viewing all with equal pleasure.
No matter where they wander, they have
No sense of duality.
They are not bothered by thirst or hunger.
If food is available, they eat—
But they do not ask for food.
Those who offer them poison and those who
Offer them milk are the same.
Those who beat them and those who love them
Are the same.

Avadhuts recognize the universe as
Father, mother, family.
They contain the entire universe
And the universe is merged in them.

110

The state of realization means
Experiencing oneness inside.
The microcosm is visible inside.
The macrocosm is seen within; it is not created.

Creation is a process of the mind—
Not of the Self.
For the mind, there is fear;
For the body, there is creation.
When the world is realized within,
There is no fear.

Those who adorn the body with gold and jewels
Know fear.
Those without ornament have no cause for sorrow,
Having equal vision.

Those who see with the physical eye
Find differences, have desires,
And are impelled to act.
Desirelessness is liberation!

Absence of desire for the fruits of action is
Self-Realization.
This is the state of the avadhut.
This is the subtle state!

One who is Self-realized has inner sight.
Having dissolved the mind,
Such a person experiences
The One in all.

All is One.
Differences belong to the gross state,
And the inner breath is indivisible.
It is One!

111

A person without a guru does not realize
The truth.
In this world, there is no effect
Without a cause.

Spiritual wisdom means seeing light
In the world's darkness.
Darkness is ignorance, light is knowledge!

Do not be a hypocrite to earn fame.

 112

One whose mind is always at one with the
Absolute is a Brahmachari.
Such a person is on the path to knowledge of God,
Even if an untouchable.

Wearing orange robes,
Carrying a walking stick or water pot,
Talking of Vedanta and
Arguing about it with everyone—
These things do not make one a swami!

113

To be fit for the name "guru"
One must renounce completely the idea
That "I am the body."

There is none higher than such a guru!
Even God is not higher than
The guru who is identified
With the Absolute.

Such a guru is a manifestation of
The bliss of universal consciousness.
Such a guru is God made manifest.

 114

What you hold in your hand has
Neither scent nor value—
Only what you receive from others.

The highest yoga is eternal bliss,
Om, the all-pervading universal sound.
The universal teacher is eternal bliss!

115

Devotion is intense, divine love.
Giving food and drink
Is neither devotion nor love—
This delusion of the mind pertains
Only to the body.
Learn to eat the subtle food.
Learn to drink the waters of discrimination.
Peace is water and settling into
The waters of peace is
The joy of yoga.

O mind!
Leave worldly delights and enjoy eternal delight.
Enter the eternal.
Run into the heart.
The Divine is in the heart.
Real joy is in the heart.
Your own liberation is in the heart.

Live in this joy!
Enter the inner and leave the outer.
Open the third eye and see the world
With equal vision.

116

If you look at ten people,
You will find that their devotion
Is not identical in nature.
If ten people are traveling on foot together
And one person sits down to rest,
The other nine soon follow.
Likewise, devotion begins with one person—
Seeing it, hearing it,
Devotion arises in others.

_____ 117

People do not get hungry at the same time
And they do not reach liberation
At the same time.
There are differences in timing.
People quarrel and debate because of
Differences in language:
One says "mittha," another "sakkare"—
But it is all sugar!
It is the same for all.
No matter how it is used,
It goes to the same place.
Those who believe in thousands of gods are
Never content.
Instead, believe in one and find happiness.
God is only one—never two!
When this is your faith, you see God in yourself.
When this is your faith, you see all as the Self.

This is the path to liberation
Where there is no enemy,
Where all are friends!
Do not court harm by believing in two.

Believe in one and reach liberation.

Return to your origin.

Understand cause and effect:

Play on life's stage and then

Return to your origin and find liberation.

Liberation does not come searching for you!

You must make the effort to seek it.

What is this liberation?

It is detachment from actions;

It is detachment from the internal state.

Not attained by any outward path,

Liberation is not different from your Self.

Liberation looks so far away to you

Because you have not really worked to reach it.

You do not reach it by running here or going there.

Search inside yourself!

Merge the mind in the higher mind;

Follow the path of subtle discrimination

To liberation.

Man makes images and calls them God.

This is ignorance!

Shake off the ignorance and

Follow the path of discrimination
To liberation in this life.
God is infinite!

There is nothing without devotion.
Your love for an object is a kind of devotion.
Trust whatever you have followed with faith
That gave results—
Do not let this belief lessen.
All creatures have devotion—it is their right.
Like water, devotion can flow in many ways,
But it is there—full—in everything.
Pure devotion is attained through
The sky of the heart.
Turned inward, pure devotion shall know the
Subtle wisdom.
There, one is without desire, without care.
Follow the path of the sushumna channel
In the subtle body and
The conscious creative energy flowing there.
This is the creative power of Shiva!
This is kundalini!
This is eternal liberation!

118

As is your devotion,
So is your liberation.

Good work brings good wages—
A little work brings only a little.

 119

Water added to a cup that is already full
Overflows.
One who is filled with perfect peace becomes
Known to all.

Such a person has no desires.
This is the highest peace,
The fullest peace.
Union.

## 120

Desireless devotion does not promise
Worldly pleasure.
Devotion is not related to nature—
Its intent is not to eliminate difficulties.
There is no relationship at all
Between devotion and difficulty.
It is not a thing of the body.
Pure devotion never turns back—
It always moves forward.
Embrace the heart firmly with pure devotion,
Hold tight with steadfast faith—
Whatever the difficulty.
By following the path of skill,
Unite devotion with Shakti.

Such a heart is purified of desire and
Joined to pure renunciation.
Let the desirelessness strengthen!
Let the senses be quieted!
Om is All, the creator of the universe,
The granter of peace.
Let your devotion be steady in this creator,

This granter of peace;
This is eternal peace, Self-luminous,
The essence of being.
Such devotion is beyond this world and
Beyond the next;
It is the mind filled with eternal delight.
This is the best devotion!

The mind filled with eternal delight is
The seed of all things.
Nourish the seed with spiritual discernment!
The mind filled with eternal delight is
Without qualities, without disease,
Without blemish, without sin.
The universal Reason,
Creator, Witness of All, the universal Being,
One in all, all knowledge, the one cause and effect,
Universal Witness, universal Guru,
Universal Father and Mother,
Om Bindu, the Om of "me-a-i"
The Supreme, the Moveable,
The Seen, the Essence.
Om! Om! Om!

121

Giving food or money to charity is not devotion.
Universal love is devotion.
Seeing God in all beings is devotion.
Looking with equal vision is devotion.

 122

When you walk in the dark,
There is fear—
But not so in daylight.

Darkness is ignorance, light is knowledge.
The guru is light!
Light is the guru!

 123

Fear is an imagination of the mind.
To the inner eye, there is no fear.
A blind man cannot describe a cart.
A person without a guru can find
No place in the world.

124

Everything comes from inside—
Not from outside!
You become evil by yourself
And you become good by yourself.

When the breath and power of Om
Is inside you, there is purity.
Evil merged in good becomes good.

 125

If you are afraid of fire,
You cannot cook a meal.
If you are afraid of water,
You cannot cross a river
Even in a boat.

There must be no fear.
For anything to be done,
First you must have courage.

126

A good person sees everyone as good.
One becomes good through personal effort.

 127

To remain in the center of the guru's glance,
The mind must be kept steady and firm—
Not flickering like the reflection of sunlight
In moving water.

 128

In the beginning, devotion may be selfish,
But in time, all desires turn toward the Self.
The whole world becomes the guru.

 129

Yoga posture is the station.
A good posture is raja yoga.

130

At birth a child is perfect and free.
At death also there is perfection and freedom.
In between there is delusion.

That which pervades in all four directions is
The One, indivisible.
Within it is the many, divisible.

 131

A child born of the womb inherits differences
Based on time.
The child's nature is affected
By the thoughts of the parents—
Whether it be devotion, deceit, anger,
Activity, desire.

Life begins when the vital breath enters the womb.
If the parents think of this world or of the next,
The child will have the same inclination.
If they think of the next world,
Sudden enlightenment is possible!

132

Young children do not think about their parents;
Only as they grow do they begin knowing
Their mother and father.
When a chicken eats,
It scratches every particle toward its feet.

As the mind develops, selfishness grows.
Every day people are born, every day people die,
But rarely is selfishness given up.

However, it is possible to give it up completely:
When identity merges
With the indivisible universal Self,
Selfishness burns to ashes.

Many kinds of food are prepared from rice.
Some are called "halva"
And some are called "ambada"—
But these dishes are not called "rice."

133

A ripe banana is sweet,
The green fruit is hard and sour;
Yet both grow on the same tree.
Only time is different.
A coconut planted in the ground
Does not produce fruit immediately.
It does not even produce the tree immediately!
First, the tender shoot appears,
Then the young sapling;
After years, the tree matures
And only then comes the fruit.

While a sapling is easily uprooted,
A tree stands firm.
So also should the mind stand firm!
Regardless of what people say to or about you,
This is what you must accomplish in this life.
Let it be your sole purpose at all costs—
Even when your head might be chopped off.
Learning to bind without rope
Is our purpose in this life.

134

The sun is reflected in both
The salty waves of the sea
And in the clear surface of a mountain lake.

Seeing things with the physical eyes
Is not enough.
You must experience the inner significance
Of the thing seen.

 135

Give up honor and pride.
Give up love of the body.
Only then can you see God everywhere
And in every being.

136

Renunciation born of seeing dead bodies
Burning in the cremation ground
Is temporary.

Desirelessness given by the guru
Should be held and cultivated.
Such renunciation leads to liberation!

This renunciation is first.
The guru is second.
Desire for guidance and initiation is third.

To practice renunciation yourself and
Experience true desirelessness
Is the highest attainment of human life!

To achieve desirelessness and
Impart it to others
Is the highest attainment of yoga!

Indivisible, it is the Tree of Peace!
Climb this tree in the head and find
Imperishable desirelessness at the top.

The first step is to renounce desire and anger.
The second step is to live in the world,
Taste its pleasures, and then renounce them.

True desirelessness is the state of
Liberation in this life.
Jivanmukti!

 137

Money, jewels, status, authority, and power
Cause fear and striving:
Fear of losing them, striving for more,
Fear of death—
For death will bring an end to the sense-pleasures.
Without them, there is no fear.

138

At the moment of death,
It is Shiva that saves you—
Not Hari, Lord of the Outer Nature.

In Shiva there is Shakti,
In Hari there is Maya.
The body is of the earth,
Its senses looking outward.

Shiva is internal, Brahmarandhra,
The sky of the heart.
This knowledge cannot be learned
From another—it must be experienced.

139

It is rare to be a millionaire.
And everyone cannot be one
At the same time because
People are rewarded according to their due.
While there is plenty of water in the sea,
How much one receives depends
On the size of the container carried to it.
Likewise, it is the residue of past actions
That determines the fruit.

Because of their past actions
Some people are interested
In the teachings of holy men.
Because of their past actions
They find no pleasure in the world.
Those so guided have no need
For special renunciations because
Desirelessness results from past actions.
For such people
Now is the time to pursue liberation!

140

Now—before you die—leave the jungle road
And follow the royal road.

On your deathbed you may suffer
If the life-force is obstructed by disease.

Now—before you die—
Purify the vital breath and consciousness!

 141

Desirelessness is like fire burning cloth:
The greater the desirelessness,
The greater the splendor from within.
The mind—not the body—
Should be firmly seated.
Without a pure mind,
How can you develop equal vision?
Without practice, how can you develop balance?
Through practice, one's subtle intelligence develops
And the desire for objects disappears.

It is difficult to give up attachments
To gold, women, and recognition.
But what is the purpose of life?

Merge the mind and the properties into One;
Become one-pointed.
Dirty linen is renewed by a washing
In soap and water.
Purify the mind in the water of
Spiritual discernment and it will be
As pure as the sky of pure consciousness!

When you first use a treadle sewing machine,
Your attention is on your hands—
Not on your legs.
Carefully place the higher mind:
Merge mind and thought in the heart-space
And attain peace.
This is eternal bliss! Nityananda!*

142

True worship is not performed by hands
Or mouth.
Action and work are not performed by hands
Or legs.
The Self is not realized by the mind.

O mind!
Act without desire for results.
Work without attachment.
Attain desirelessness and see all equally.

143

From one coconut tree come thousands
Of coconuts.
But if the trunk of the coconut tree is cut,
The fruits cease.

Attachment is like the trunk:
Sever it with the ax of discrimination and
Find peace.

The properties of harmony, balance, and
Inner peace come from non-attachment.
A steady mind yields perfect balance.

Truth is like letters engraved in stone—
The talk of ordinary men is like letters
Written in chalk.

144

On a single mango tree,
Not all fruits grow and ripen at the same time.

First there is the tender young fruit,
Which in its own time ripens and is good to eat.

Be like the mango fruit—
At peace in everything!

 145

A brahmin is one who has experienced
The joy of the Absolute.
Maya is transient.
O Hari, burn the ego!
One who has destroyed the mind has
Destroyed delusion.
Maya is not the Lord—
Shiva is the Lord!

Everyone knows there is butter in milk.
When milk has been boiled,
Butter can be churned out.
But so few take the butter.

The milk is bhakti—love and devotion.
Heating the milk over fire is the power
Of discrimination.
The vessel for discrimination is the higher mind.
The fire is the fire of yoga.
In this fire, the six enemies of the body—
Anger, desire, envy, passion, greed, delusion—
Are destroyed and the butter extracted.

 146

When gold is melted in fire,
Its dross is burned away,
Leaving it glowing with lustrous purity.

To purify yourself,
Desire, passion, and anger
Must be destroyed within.

All activity takes place within.
All exertion is directed within.
The mind does not remain in one state!

147

An object buried in filth has no value.
But if it is extracted and cleaned,
Everyone can benefit.
You do not throw away a diamond found in
The mire!

 148

When a ripe coconut is freshly picked
And opened,
The kernel inside is closely bound to the
Inside of the shell.
Any damage to the outer shell also damages
The kernel.

But when a coconut is left on the tree
Or exposed to the sun,
The water inside evaporates and
The dried kernel separates from the shell,
Making a noise when shaken.

Similarly, one must realize that the inner Self
Is distinct from the body.
The fire of this knowledge burns up
All shortcomings,

Like a coconut whose water is burned off
By the sun,
The mind then shines like
Purified gold.

 149

The glow of pure gold is revealed
Through the heat of fire.
Likewise, the inner world is made luminous
Through the heat of concentration.
Let the world be illuminated within!
Follow the way of the Higher Mind—
Of spiritual discernment,
Of subtle discrimination,
Of wisdom, of a steady mind.

Perfect one-pointedness!
This is understanding that approaches
The Thought of the Self.
Experience does not come from words,
Words flow from experience.
The tree is in the seed, the seed is not in the tree.
Man is not in the world, the world is in man
And subject to man.

Speak the words your mind thinks,
Let there be no deceit or malice in your heart.
Deceive no one, hate no one.
In the company of others, live always within
And keep the mind one-pointed.
The deceitful heart is like the face of the sun
During monsoon:
At times, a star breaks through the clouds
And shines with glory—
But in minutes it is hidden again.

Man's nature changes within five minutes.
The ego-mind falls into the Self
Like a shooting star falls from the sky.
The sky of the heart is not visible
To the physical eye—
Only to the subtle eye.
Through thought, know the Thought!
Through sound, know the Sound!
Through mind, know the Mind!

Low activities and a mean disposition indicate
A lack of good sense.
This lack of good sense marks a pariah.
Laughing at and mocking others,
Lying, pride, jealousy—
These are characteristics of a pariah.
Not dark skin and black clothes!
Not poverty and hunger!
Do a turban, a wristwatch, and a suit indicate
An admirable man?

No!  A pariah is a selfish person who sees
Nothing but differences.

One who does not realize
The truth of Vedanta is no man.
Like a well-trained horse,
One who studies carefully
Finds liberation in this life.
But one who studies like a wild elephant
Finds only delusion.

 151

Even the worst sinner can be changed into a
Knower of Truth
In an instant.

There is no sun when there are clouds,
But the moment the clouds scatter—
The sun is visible!

Om is the City of Peace, the form of Peace.
Give respect and gratitude to Om.

152

Board the train for Kashi.
Travel to Shivanandapuri,
The city of the bliss of Shiva,
In the country of Shanti, Peace.
The journey ends at Brahmanandapuri,
The city of the bliss of God.*


153

Look to God residing in the sky of the heart.
Yes! You must see God in your own heart.
To see God with the inner eye is to experience
Eternal bliss.
It is delusion to mistake a stone image for God.
All pain, all sorrow are delusion.

Praise God within!
Praise God in your heart!
Praise God in your head!

Discover the Self's secret that is
Eternal delight.

Yes! You must know that secret.
Look into your heart with the inner eye and
Discover the royal road.
Leave the downward path and
Take the middle path.
To adorn the external body without knowing
The inner secret
Is the downward path.

 154

Nobody wants a tree without fruit.
Why is man called "man"?
Because he has the reflective power of mind.
Use your mind to get knowledge and then
Unite with peace.
Finally become one with the power and
Sound of Om.
Liberation and eternal life are only possible
When you give up the idea that "I am the body."
Only then can you realize the Self.

It is very difficult for those
Who think "I am the body"
To see the Self.
Those who cling to the body-idea cannot gain
Even the smallest bit of peace—
Even by performing a spiritual discipline
For a thousand years.

Anyone can bathe in a river and cleanse the body.
A brahmin, a pariah, a child—
Whoever bathes will be cleansed.
The spirit in all is also the same—
Only the exterior forms differ.
Chilies and watermelons can grow in the
Same field, even though their natures differ.
Only those who sit near the fire will feel
Its warmth—
Not those who sit in water.

Peace is cool, like water.
One's nature is like fire.
Food must be prepared before you are hungry.

Know the duties of a householder
Before you become a householder.
The householder should be equally attracted
To the inner and the outer and
Distinguish clearly between cause and effect.

 155

It is futile to run after the horse—
Ride it instead!
Bind the horse's feet and mount quickly.
It is also futile to chase the pleasures of
The world—
Instead, keep your mind free of attachments.

As water slips off an umbrella,
So the idea that "I am the doer" should pass
From you.
The householder must be like the calf
Dedicated to the temple and offered
To God.

You cannot say that the one who does the
Offering is closer to God than the one
Who does not.
A light placed before a thousand people
Shines on them all—without distinction.
Anyone may take it!

In light, there is no darkness;
In darkness, there is no light—
It is either one or the other.
Let your nature be like the sun
And the mind as cool as the moon.

156

Fire, water, earth, and air
Are available to and used by everyone.

Water flowing from a pipe can be used
By the brahmin, the untouchable,
And the child with no distinction.*

 157

It is not that "this one" has more
And another has less.
The faculties of mind, ears, nose, hands, eyes
Are the same for everyone.*

158

To hew a tree into planks,
One moves the saw up and down.
So let it be with the breath—
Induced into the higher mind and always
Moved upward.

It takes great effort to roll a huge rock
Up a hill and no effort to let it
Roll down again—
Difficult to ascend and easy to descend.
Likewise it is difficult for the vital breath
To leave the body's cage.

To receive something is easy;
To return what has been given is difficult.
Nevertheless, those who do not return what
They have been given are less than men—
They are animals without virtue.

159

Find out who you are, look deeply and find out.
"Other" is not the truth, cultivate the "same."
Reach deeply within for the secret.
The sense of separateness is not the truth!

Words and actions should show "sameness."
Burn the physical sight—and look!
It is the sense of separateness
That causes suffering at the time of death.

 160

With faith,
Stabilize the breath of life in an
Upward direction.
This is the path to liberation.

Yoga is union.
The eternal spirit dwells in the cave of the body.
When the two merge—that is yoga.

When the mind and the higher mind become
One—that is yoga.
When the eternal spirit follows the path of
Subtle discrimination and enters
The sky of the heart—that is yoga.

Devotion, reflection, power all merge
And become Om.
The ego melts into the Om sound
Like camphor melts in fire.
The mental processes merge in the Self.

Place the mind in the higher mind
Like a child placed in the cradle and rocked.
Know who you are.

 161

Draw the Om sound inside with the breath
Just as you draw water from a well.
And like dropping the bucket for a refill,
Release the exhalation with Om.

162

If you do not concentrate on the breath,
There is no aim, no state,
No intelligence, no fulfillment.
Concentrate!

Think without losing concentration.
Concentrate on the inbreath and the outbreath;
Draw the breath evenly, properly.
Concentrate on the sound of the breath,
Breathe and concentrate on the internal sound,
Have faith in that sound, and breathe in.
Breathe deeply and more deeply.
Breathe so the internal sound is audible to
The ears and think of nothing else.
Eating, drinking, walking, standing—
Such things do not elevate the soul!

Do your own work—
Do not desire to eat what others have cooked.
With faith, do what you have to do.

163

The heart of Vedanta is prana,
Bringing the breath under complete control.
Vedanta is knowledge of the Indivisible.

Vedic mantras are not to be uttered
By the tongue, but from the throat.
One who knows this secret is a brahmin.

The sound of Om itself
Constitutes the Vedas.
It is the light of divine wisdom,
The fire of intuition.

Vedanta has no form;
It is indivisible, changeless.
It is identical to the Self.
Right utterance of Veda is perfect
Concentration of the mind.*

164

If the breath is not harmonious and rhythmical,
The inner fire is reduced to a dull glow.
Without this fire, food is not digested properly.

When the free flow of air and energy
Is obstructed,
The imbalance leads to all disease.
Water cannot flow through a blocked pipe.

 165

Without control of the breath,
One cannot be a sannyasi or a yogi.
A boat without a rudder cannot be steered.

Allow the breath to move upward freely.
To push a stone uphill requires great effort—
But to roll it downhill requires none.
With concentration, it is the same.

It is easy to take birth but difficult
To leave this body.
Discover the river's source—
It is useless to seek it after it has joined the sea.
To a tree, its central root is most important.
All others are secondary.

Lift a chair and witness your breath
Move upward;
This is the seat of vital breath.
When cooking, both flame and smoke
Move upward.
In a chimney, the movement is upward.
In the sky of the heart, the movement
Of breath is also upward.

This upward movement brings joy!
Without it, blood does not circulate.
When a river is dammed,
The flow of water stops.
The physical body's dam is made of the
Three humors: wind, phlegm, and bile.

 167

There are three kinds of breathing:
Inhalation, retention, and exhalation.
These processes are internal with
Nothing taken from outside.

In the practice of pranayama,
The breath is controlled and becomes centered
In the sushumna channel of the subtle body.
In this state, joy and bliss flow within.

O Brahmananda!
Forget the world! Forget the body!
There is only the world beyond—only Brahmaloka,
Only God.

The best cobras have the internal breath,
Listening attentively to the sweet music of
The flute.
One who has realized the Self
Loves all people and all things
As deeply as the cow loves her calf.
This is "same-sightedness" or equal vision.

There can be no house without doors,
No cooking without utensils.
A dog will eat happily from a golden dish or
From a stone trough.
A bird thinks only of today's needs—
Not of tomorrow's.
A seed kept in a box will never grow.
But if placed in soil,
This same seed will sprout and yield fruit.

You must practice! You must experience!
You yourself are responsible for your own
Happiness or misery.

169

There is no house without doors,
No hot water without fire,
No fire without air,
No life without food.

Without the breath of life
One cannot live
Even for a few seconds.

 170

Do not be satisfied
With the leftover scraps of a feast.
Insist on a fresh serving of food!

Only by doing can you enjoy
The bliss that flows from
Experiencing the Divine.

171

Those who do not breathe
Through mouth or nostrils
Have no desires—
Their breathing is purely internal.
They draw the breath upward
To the Brahmarandhra chakra
At the top of the head
Where the ida and pingala channels meet.

They realize themselves as the Self
And look upon all things as Self.
This is the kingdom of the Self
And the true goal of human life.
The light of life is the life-force—
The breath of life.
Freedom is the capital.
The Lord of the government is the Self.
And swarajya is one's own Shakti
To be kept in one's possession.

Total freedom is neither a hill nor gold.
Keeping both desire and anger under
Perfect control brings total freedom.
Let both speech and action be the same.*

 172

Suffering given by God is not suffering.
Grief given by God is not grief.
It is a delusion of the mind.

There is grief at birth
And there is grief at the end.
Man comes from his mother's womb
With tears in his eyes.*

 173

Human beings are the highest of all creatures—
No incarnation is higher!
And those who think deeply
And fix firmly on the Self
Are the very highest.

174

If an evil person falls in the well,
What should you do?
Pull him up!
Do not think that the bad will always be bad—
Show them the right road.

 175

In the beginning,
Before perfect peace is attained,
Maya's play is great.
Wherever you turn, there is the serpent.

In the beginning,
When you sit to practice,
You may feel as heavy as a mountain,
As if you are leaving the ground,
As if you are sitting in the sea,
As if hot water were being poured over you,
As if you were sitting on high and observing,
As fine and subtle as the point of a needle,
As insubstantial as a leaf...

You may not know whether you are
Walking, talking, or sitting.
At times, all feelings cease, leaving you
As still and rooted as the coconut tree.
You may look about and see only actors
In a play.
You may see black faces.
In perfect peace, all is infinite white light;
Light in darkness, darkness in light;
The universe in darkness,
In the universe—light.
At times, everything may seem like a movie
On a screen.
At other moments, only being
In the bliss of consciousness.
Questions may arise such as:
"Why have I come into this world?"
"Where am I going?"
"What is my duty?"
Coming down is not permanent—but rising,
Step by step, to the upper story is!

All that is seen,
All that is heard,
All that is done—
Such things are like a net that cannot be severed.
Listen!
All-penetrating Om is the all-penetrating
Universal sound.

 176

An ear would be of no use in place of an eye.
Work given to the legs should be done
By the legs.
And hands are not suited for walking—
They have their own work,
Which does not include thinking.
Thinking is done by the brain.
Likewise, each of us must do that
For which we are suited!

177

Hunger is not satisfied by the smell of food—
You must eat the food to be satisfied!
Experience is necessary.
When you have experienced truth,
No one can oppose you.

You cannot experience sugar's sweetness by
Holding it in your hand—
You must put it in your mouth.
This is experience.
Knowledge gained from books leaves room
For doubt and questions.

Experience is certain.

 178

After first rehearsing in private,
The actor then performs his role for others.

Conduct your initial practices in secret—
Later this is not necessary.

179

Cow's milk never tastes bitter.
A statue does not speak.
Merely visiting holy places like Kashi
And Rameshwar does not bring liberation.
First silence the mind and establish it in the Self,
Then concentrate deeply with
Spiritual discernment.

Stone or clay statues and ritualistic worship
Do not reveal God.
If the true significance of the statue
Or ceremony is not understood,
Liberation is impossible.
Human birth is the effect—giving it back
Is the cause.

Comprehending properly,
Removing the primordial ignorance,
And dedicating this life to seeking the
True source—
This leads to the peace of liberation!

180

Holding sugar in the palm of your hand does
Not lead to knowledge of its sweetness.
Only by eating sugar can its sweetness
Be known.

Merely repeating holy names like
Rama, Krishna, and Govinda,
Even for a thousand years,
Cannot bring liberation.

Mantra must be repeated
With full knowledge, devotion, and
Concentration.

 181

Abstain from gross sleep.
Instead sleep in the subtle state,
Resting in concentration
On the internal breath.

182

In the beginning of practice, sleep less.
When eating sparingly, do not bathe in cold water;
Frequent cold water baths affect blood circulation.

183

For liberation and wisdom,
Age is no consideration.
This is the moment.

If you are hungry, you should eat.
If you are not hungry, you should wait.
The hunger for devotion must be intense.

The bigger the fire, the sooner the water boils.
Intense faith is the heat.
Peace is like ice in the head,
Filling the inside and overflowing to the outside.

Fully satisfied, the mind becomes pure.
This peace, this contentment, cost nothing—
Not even a penny for charity.

When you are filled with this peace,
Those around you also benefit.
When it begins in you, it also begins in others.

Even among thousands,
If one person has this peace,
Others can enjoy a part of it.

When entering a crowd,
A holy man should have the peace of
The hunter approaching a tiger.

To live in the world, a holy man must have
Great calm, great peace.
Peace is of great help in moving
Among thousands of people.

184

Fire consumes anything and everything,
Making no distinction between good or evil.

Those who work can consume anything,
Their active fire enabling them to eat and
Digest anything.
Those who do not work do not know what
Must be done—they get indigestion.

Sleep in moderation.
Do not eat on a full stomach.
In all things be regular.

 185

There are no strict dietary rules.
Eat satisfying food, and in its consumption
Be regular and moderate.
Fill half the stomach with food,
A quarter with water, and
Leave a quarter empty.
Do not indulge in too much sleep.

186

Many different things are brought to a fair.
Peace can be pursued in many ways.
Amid thousands, remain steadfast.

As an airplane moves without the help of the earth,
So you must move without concern for the body.
Plant the conviction "I am not the body"
Firmly in your heart.

A traveler,
Weary from walking under the hot sun,
Forgets his fatigue as soon as he rests
On a shaded hillside.
So a person who rests in the knowledge of
The Supreme forgets his worldly troubles.

Once you enter the cool, you forget the heat.
Likewise, thoughts of "I" and "mine"
Are forgotten.
No umbrella is needed inside the house—
Only outside.

When you sit inside the house and lock
All the doors, you see nothing but the inside.
It is only when you open the doors
That the outside is seen.
Learn to open and shut the doors of the senses.

When the warehouse is locked, all business stops.
When the senses are shut down,
There is no difference between inside and outside.

Take care with the senses—
They are like a horse that must be reined.

Keep your attention fixed on the senses—
As fixed as a nail in the wall.

Keep your attention above the neck—
Never below the neck.

 187

Two or one?
From a distance
A train and the tracks appear connected.
But really they are separate.

The track is pre-set by one's gross nature.
The train is moved by the steam of
Subtle discrimination.
Examine the connection
Between body and spirit:
It is via the higher mind
And its subtle intelligence
That peace is attained!

As the railroad cars join to form one train,
So let the individual and the Self be connected.
Sever the bonds of all physical qualities and
Let the Self incarnate reach eternal liberation!

188

If water is heated in a tightly closed vessel,
The heat's energy stays inside.
Water flows from the pump making the
Om sound.

Abandon the wild jungle path and take
The royal road—
Take the downward-moving energy
And move it upward.
The mind should know its place!

 189

Changing the outward appearance
Without realizing the truth within
Does not change karma.

One does not become a renunciate
By assuming the clothing and
Mannerisms of a monk
While keeping deceit within.

Parasite! Hypocrite!
Speak what is in your mind!
Act as you speak!

A person who attains unity of
Body, mind, and speech,
Whose actions fit his words,
And whose words are true to the inner Self,

This one is the real renunciate,
The yogi, the Self-realized one,
The paramahamsa who can distinguish
Real from unreal.

The renunciate gives up desire.
One who gives up desire is the guru.*

190

Sat-Being is the indivisible subtle thought.
Chit-Consciousness is always changing.
When they merge, the result is bliss!

When the Self incarnate
Joins the Supreme Self,
The result is bliss!

Yogananda, paramananda, satchitananda,
Brahmananda, nityananda!

# Commentary

## SUTRA I

*Atman* is used interchangeably with *Self* in these Sutras. Atman refers to the universal Self that manifests as a proliferation of rays emanating from itself. These rays are not different from the nature of their source, but only take on the appearance of separateness. *Kundalini* is the Supreme conscious energy manifesting as an individuated person (*jivatman*). *Paramatman* is the Absolute. Both are Atman. It is the merging of Atman into Atman, like the merging of waves into water, that is the goal of spiritual practice: the union of the individual and the Divine. The Absolute, the Supreme, Paramatman, Brahman, the Self are all synonymous with Atman in these Sutras.

The image of *chidakash* is also central to Nityananda's teaching as given in these Sutras; the word is formed of the roots *chit*, consciousness, and *akasha*, space or sky, and is thus poetically translated as the sky of consciousness. It is synonymous with *hridayakasha*, sky of the heart. When the original Kanarese edition of Nityananda's words was prepared for printing, his devotees asked him to suggest a title. He replied simply that the words had come from chidakash. Thus the work was entitled *Chidakash Gita*.

As discussed in the Introduction, chidakash is an experience; it is a state of consciousness in which perception is objectless and limitlessly vast, a state in which the individual and the universal are in complete union. In various disciplines, this experience of Oneness may be called *samadhi, turiya, nirvana,* or *shunya.* Surface distinctions notwithstanding, there is no essential difference among these terms.

Nityananda also called this "heart-space of the Atman" the Brahmarandhra, and the sahasrara chakra, the thousand-petaled lotus; for him, these were all the same. They all refer to that secret point in the head where the light of consciousness shines in its purest form. When an individual's kundalini energy is completely roused, it merges into this place in the head. The awakening that occurs in our understanding at that time reveals our complete and total unity in the Divine. When we realize that we are in God and that God is in us, then there is nothing outside of us. All knowledge is accessible from within.

## Sutra 6

The three primary gunas are *sattva, rajas,* and *tamas.* Collectively, they are *Prakriti,* cosmic Nature, the "stuff" of all manifestation. They are simply three different forms of manifestation: still, dynamic, and dense. Sattva guna is pure space, pure light, pure peace. Tamas guna is the opposite; it is density, darkness, and inertia. Rajas guna is fire and dynamic activity. They are at once hierarchical and not hierarchical, since the peace exists in everyone, everyone has dynamic capability, and there is also inertia in everyone. It is just another way of speaking about the spectrum of manifestation. Tamas guna (inertia, thickness) is one end of the spectrum, sattva guna (pure light) is the opposite end, and rajas guna is the meeting of the two, for when pure light and pure density meet, the result is fire. Yet upon reaching sattva guna, there is no more hierarchy. In the pure state of sattva guna, everything is seen as equal; there is no separate mind, no chakras, no nadis—nothing is separate. Sattva guna is pure and perfect balance.

In man, these gunas are found in a state of instability. Sattva causes moments of inspiration, meditative calm, quiet joy, and disinterested affection. Rajas brings out constructive activity, energy, enthusiasm, and physical courage as well as ambition and rage. Tamas is associated with the lowest qualities such as sloth, stupidity, helpless despair, obstinancy and the like.

## Sutra 13

The source of liberation is pure consciousness, the awareness of our real Self. The linga in the head is the seat of this pure consciousness. The linga is a stone symbol in the shape of an egg which is the iconography for Shiva as Absolute Potential. It is egg-shaped to represent the unity of the universe—its internal consistency and its formless presence in all directions. Thus, the linga has no corners or edges; it is all Om. It has no face because pure consciousness has no face. The linga in the head corresponds to the *medulla oblongata*, or brain stem, at the junction between brain and spinal column. This is the still point in the head, the place where the ida, pingala, and sushumna meet. For Nityananda, the Shiva linga, the Brahmarandhra, the prana linga, the sahasrara are all the same: the Abode of Shiva, the doorway to God.

## Sutra 14

The cities of Kashi and Haridwar were both popular places of pilgrimage for devout Hindus wishing to be freed of sin. However, Nityananda asserts that the only truly effective pilgrimage is the inner journey. The nine gates of Haridwar refer to the chakras, while the ritual sacrifice (*yajna*) is the awakening of the inner fire of kundalini which brings the experience of supreme happiness.

## Sutra 15

The distinction between *manas* and *buddhi* is often made in these Sutras. The terms have very precise technical meanings, but often in the Sutras, a broader meaning is implied. (See the Glossary.) Here, manas refers to the gross expression of the mind through thoughts, concepts, and feelings. This aspect of what we call our mind is limited in every way, and it always gets us into trouble by thinking we want this, we want that, we want something else. Manas reaches for pleasure and seeks to avoid pain. Buddhi, on the other hand, is intelligence. It is farsighted, it is not concerned about truth. In the face of every difficulty and complexity, buddhi manifests our own and everyone else's highest best interest. Nityananda called this intelligence subtle discrimination and spiritual discernment.

Nityananda was fond of the railway and often used railroad analogies in his talks. During the twenties and thirties, he spent considerable time traveling by train between Mangalore and Kanhangad, often riding in the engine car. As the engineers came to know him, it became the custom for trains to whistle when passing the Kanhangad Ashram.

## Sutra 16

Shiva-Shakti is pure consciousness, the union of pure potential and pure energy that forms the dynamic stillness at the heart of the universe. Kundalini and prana are components of this highest of forces; they relate to Shiva-Shakti like body and arm relate to the pure consciousness of being.

## SUTRA 17

Nadis are the channels of creative energy, of conscious energy. Within the Self, the vibration of Omkar interacts with itself and gives rise to different currents, just as the constant movement of the ocean interacts with variances in depth and temperature to give rise to the currents that flow within it. The currents, though individual, are still water, they are not different in essence from the ocean itself. Our physical being can be compared to a current in the ocean of Omkar, and the nadis are the channels for the flow of this conscious energy that is the essence of the mind, the emotions, and the physical body. The nadis *are* the subtle body. And it is awareness of these nadis that leads us to the recognition of our true nature: the Self.

As Nityananda describes, there are three major nadis. The conscious, creative energy of life itself flows unceasingly through these channels. As listed in the Sutras, these nadis are associated with colors as well as with celestial bodies.

## Sutra 18

In accordance with the highest and most secret sacred texts, Nityananda distinguishes between the chakra systems above the neck and below the neck, relating them to hatha yoga and raja yoga respectively. For him, hatha yoga and the chakras below the neck relate to the body and the mind, the material world and its attainments. They represent duality, accomplishment, and effort.

To Nityananda, raja yoga is no effort; it is non-dual and indivisible. Thus, the chakras above the neck refer not only to the psychic mechanism but more importantly to the experience of pure, endless, spacious consciousness; consciousness that is unlimited in any way. Raja yoga is the continuous, unbroken awareness of the Absolute.

## Sutra 20

Scholars differ about the correct translation of *shunya*. While the common translation is "nothingness" or "void," some prefer the precision of "the absence of subject-object relation." In either case, it is simply another word, usually associated with Buddhism, to describe the super-conscious state.

## SUTRA 36

To illustrate the point that for one who sees the Atman "actions are like inaction," a story is told of the great sage Vyasa, who is credited with recording the eighteen Puranas and the Mahabharata, as well as editing the Vedas. Early one evening, Vyasa was sitting on the banks of the river Jumna, watching its swirling rise to the high-water mark. He was approached by an anxious group of milkmaids, who could find no way to cross the turbulent river. They recognized Vyasa as a great sage and asked that he petition the river to let them cross. The sage asked if they had anything in their pots. They offered him all the curds they had, and he ate all that they offered. Then he stood up and spoke to the river: "If I have not eaten anything, make a passage for these milkmaids." The river responded immediately. Since they had watched Vyasa eat, the milkmaids were totally baffled until they realized that it was merely the outer body that had eaten. The true Vyasa was identified with the Atman all the while and was not affected.

## SUTRA 38

The Ramayana is a Hindu epic that incorporates history, mythology, and spiritual philosophy. It is very popular throughout India; in many villages the re-enactment of its stories continues to be a major yearly event. Thus, the characters and symbolism of the epic are familiar to Indians, educated and rural alike.

Here, the epic is used as an allegory. Just as Sita married Rama and was ever with him, so the mind must be constantly absorbed in the Self. Just as the faithful Lakshmana remained with Rama and Sita in thought and deed, so also the devotee must long always for union with the Self. The ten senses—five of perception and five of action—are Ravana's ten faces. The mind (Sita) is seduced away from the Self (Rama) by the ten senses (Ravana) and held captive. Sita must be rescued by Lakshmana, who stands for *shraddha* (intense faith and constant attention), and by Hanuman, representing intense devotion and also pranayama, which mutually act and react on each other. Krishna is also a name of God that refers to cosmic consciousness.

## SUTRA 39

The vitality of Life itself is like a resonance that has many chords in it, chords that interact with each other to give rise to all appearances and forms, to the whole material universe. At its essence, these chords are nothing but vibration, sound, mantra. In the universe, the supreme conscious energy of God, as the Supreme word (*Paravac*), is the Supreme Mantra: the source of all mantra and of all manifestation. In the individual, the natural pulsation of the physical breath and the natural pulsation of the subtle breath (*prana*) is mantra.

## Sutra 42

When you raise desire to its highest level (that is, if you focus desire on the Divine), then you automatically cultivate love and devotion and subsequently gain release from the pain and suffering of the cycles of birth, death, and rebirth. It is a conscious process. When your energy is scattered about in the form of many different desires, little can be accomplished. Weave together all these small, petty desires and bind them into one very high, powerful desire to see God. This convergence of energy requires that you be filled with love and devotion. Then that love and devotion will slowly reveal to you the vision of the Lord. Love and devotion are totally important.

That is why I would say the most important thing in spiritual growth is the connection between you and the Divine. It is never one thing or the other, it is always what is in the middle. That is true one hundred percent of the time. If you ask is it this or is it that, is it *samsara* or is it liberation, the answer is always: "Neither." It is what is in the middle.

## Sutra 45

In the combined deity Hari-Hara, Hari is Vishnu and Hara is Shiva in their aspects as part of the Hindu trinity. This god-pair therefore is being used by Nityananda in a special, more limited context. In this sutra, Hari can be taken to mean force, or chit-shakti (mind-energy), that must be dissolved in its source (Hara) in order to reach the One (Paramashiva).

## Sutra 49

According to the Upanishads, the three states are waking, dream, and deep sleep. Yet in this sutra Nityananda lists sleep as the first state. The reference is to being asleep to the soul. That is, we may be constitutionally awake, but if we are not aware of our real Self, we are spiritually asleep. Hence the exhortation in the Katha Upanishad: "Arise, awake, and stop not till the goal is reached."

In the state of "no mind," sensations, ideas, and time have ceased. The *jnani* is described in the Bhagavad Gita as having his mind dead to the touch of the external and alive to the bliss of the eternal Absolute. To see all things equally is to see the Self in all things and all things within the Self; to be able to see the common factor, the soul or essence, through the multiplicity of forms.

The recollected mind is awake
In the knowledge of the Atman,
which is dark night to the ignorant.
The ignorant are awake in their sense-life
which they think is day-light;
To the seer it is darkness.

Being always "awake in the knowledge of the Atman," the jnani is not affected by the phenomenal sunrise and sunset.

## SUTRA 53

Once the Self is realized there is no other knowledge to be gained. The Katha Upanishad calls this the "knowledge by knowing which all else is known."

The truth of this statement was manifested by Nityananda time after time. He could casually describe a scene from ancient scriptures as if it were taking place right now, or a scene currently happening anywhere in the world as though it were unfolding right before him. In 1940, when Hitler was surging through Europe, someone asked him who would win the war. He replied that Shakti (then held to be represented by Britain) would win in the end. He described Hitler as a great destructive force capable of causing even greater damage, were it not for his lack of faith in the Divine. This lack of faith, Nityananda would say, was the chink in Hitler's armor that would lead to his delusion and destruction. Commenting on Churchill's capability, he used the analogy of the coconut to define his brain power, by saying that his "kernel" was very thick. As described in *Nityananda: The Divine Presence* (Rudra Press, 1984) even Nityananda's offhand opinions on personalities like Mountbatten and Gandhi, and on world events like India's Independence, always proved correct.

## Sutra 79

Nityananda was considered eccentric and even mad in his early days in South Kanara, particularly by the educated and by officials. Whether this aphorism refers to such comments is not known. However, many great mystics have been treated as mad by their contemporaries. For them, on the other hand, absorbed as they are in eternity, all appears the same—mad or clever, sinner or saint. (See also Sutra 31.)

## Sutra 85

Quieting the tongue is not the real silence. Real silence consists of stilling all thought and immersing the mind in Self-knowledge. Concentrating the mind in the sushumna, at the meeting place of the ida and pingala nadis, is the correct practice of silence. It is only through such silence that one can practice yoga and obtain results.

## Sutra 102

Nityananda says that the guru who initiates an aspirant is the "guru of cause," elsewhere called the secondary guru. He is differentiating between the physical teacher, who can *show* the seeker the road to Self-realization, and the "guru of action," who actually walks that road. This action guru, also called the primary guru, resides within the individual, for the action guru is nothing other than the Self of all.

## Sutra 141

Nityananda used to say that the three K's were the real obstructions (*upadhis*) on the way to perfection. In Kanarese, these K's were *kanaka*, gold or greed; *kaanta*, women or lust; and *keerti*, desire for name and fame. He used to say that these were obstructions in ascending order, becoming both more subtle and more difficult to overcome. Many, he said, would overcome the first two only to be tripped up by the desire for recognition and fame.

## Sutra 152

Kashi is one of the ancient names for the city of Benares, also called Varanasi. Kashi means "City of Light" and so, "City of Shiva." It is one of the most holy cities in India; it is said that one who dies in Benares is freed from the cycle of birth and rebirth.

The suffix "-puri" means "abode" and hence village or city.

To reach Benares, you board a train that proceeds steadily toward that destination. To reach the state of chidakash (pure and unbounded awareness), you must also proceed steadily by regular practice aimed toward your goal.

## SUTRA 156

Creative energy, Shakti, the essential knowledge: these are freely available to everyone.

Nityananda often spoke against the rigidities of the caste system. These rigidities, however, have produced some amazing compensations. One famous story concerns the great saint Kanakadasa, who was not permitted into the Krishna temple at Udipi because of his low birth. Few recognized the spiritual greatness of the saint and judged him only by his outer appearance and by the low caste to which his body belonged. Since he was not allowed to enter the shrine, the saint went around to the rear of the temple to pray, peering through a small peephole in the compound wall to catch a glimpse of the statue within. In response to Kanakadasa's sincere devotion, the statue turned 180 degrees to oblige the saint! Even to this day, the temple faces east while the statue faces west.

## SUTRA 157

Nityananda never referred to himself in the first person, instead he would say "this one" or "this place."

## SUTRA 163

Prana is the life-force, the vital air, which is a manifestation of the supreme consciousness. Vedanta is here used as "end of knowledge" or "fullness of knowledge."

From the ancient Hindu Rig Veda through the Christian Gospel According to St. John, there has been an emphasis on the Word and an identification of the Word with God. The ancient rishis studied carefully the effect of sound on the chakras. As a result of their investigation into the potencies of sound and the human voice, they also discovered that the sound "Om" vibrates throughout the cosmos. Sanskrit therefore was formulated as an essentially phonetic language, with its fifty characters having a vibratory correspondence with the fifty mystic "petals" of the chakras.

## SUTRA 171

"Those who do not breathe through the mouth or nostrils" are those people who have the awareness of the body as an extension of the highest creative energy of the Self. People think that consciousness arises because of and out of the body, but the reverse is true: the body arises from consciousness. The gross physical breath is a simple manifestation of the dynamic pulsation of the creative force that is the breath of life in all.

Nityananda's use of the term *swaragya* is interesting because of its political ramifications; it was a popular term during India's struggle for independence in the 1940s. His easy familiarity with both the term and its connotations confirms that Nityananda was quite aware of the external situation.

## Sutra 172

To renounce delusion requires renouncing grief and suffering as well. In the final analysis, renouncing delusion means giving up the selfishness of "me" and "mine." It is said that the ant would rather die on a heap of sugar that leave it, and the moth will burn in the fire of the light rather than fly into the dark and survive. An advanced yogi who had been very wealthy at the time of renunciation was praised by his disciples in later years for the greatness of his renunciation of so much wealth. The yogi answered that it was the worldly who were the real renunciates and not he, for they had renounced the whole (God) for the part (world), whereas he had renounced the part for the whole.

When the mind is merged in the Self, the result is the experience of bliss. As the individual soul becomes fully conscious of the Absolute from which it is evolved, the perfection and fullness of all is experienced:

> Om. That is perfect. This is perfect.
> From the perfect springs the perfect.
> If the perfect is taken from the perfect,
> only the perfect remains.
>
> —Upanishads

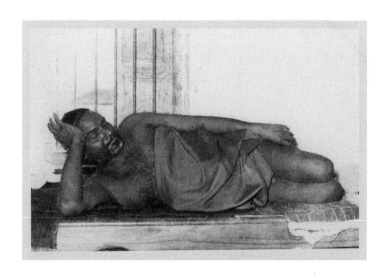

# Glossary

This glossary was developed to accompany the first American edition of Nityananda's oral teachings published as the *Nitya Sutras: The Revelations of Nityananda from the Chidakash Gita* (Rudra Press, 1985). In the present volume, in an attempt to make the sutras more accessible to the Western Reader, much of the Sanskrit has been eliminated and the meaning of terms inserted in its stead. Nonetheless, because the importance and power of the original Sanskrit cannot be denied, the glossary is included here as an aid to those who wish to delve more deeply into the words actually spoken by Nityananda.

These definitions are limited to the specific context of this book and do not claim to be authoritative. Sanskrit scholars will find certain transliteration inconsistencies, most notably in the use of the final "a" as in "Akash/a." Usage in this volume varies, since reproductions of Nityananda's speech have typically reproduced the dropped-vowel spoken form.

*agni:* fire; one of the five gross elements of the physical world: earth, water, fire air, and ether or akasha.

*ajna chakra:* a major chakra, located between the eyebrows in the subtle body; symbolized as a two-petaled lotus.

*akash/a:* lit., the sky; (1) symbol of pure consciousness, also translated as the sky or the infinite; (2) the subtlest of the five elements into which all elements are ultimately resolved, ether.

*anahata:* (1) anahata chakra is the heart chakra; (2) anahata shabda is the sound of Om heard when the kundalini has risen to the heart chakra; the unstruck sound.

*ananda:* transcendent bliss, spiritual ecstasy, delight; the essential principle of joy unaffected by worldly objects.

*Arjuna:* hero of the Mahabharata; the teaching of the Bhagavad Gita was given to him by Krishna.

*Atman:* the Self; spirit; eternal principle present in the heart of every living being. See also jivatman and paramatman.

*atmananda:* the perfect joy of the Self.

*asana:* posture or seat.

*avadhut/a:* a great mystic-renunciate who has risen above body-consciousness, duality, and conventional standards. The avadhut is described in the Bhagavatam as one who is free from the consciousness of the ego, roaming free like a child over the face of the earth.

*bandh:* from "bandhana" meaning "bondage," colloquially used to mean "shut down," as in general strike.

*Benares:* (also Banares and Banaras), now most often called by its ancient name of Varnasi because here the two rivers Varuna and Asi meet; the city's other ancient name is Kashi, meaning City of Light or City of Shiva. It is a very holy place for Hindus, for it is thought that to die in Benares, to be burned on its sacred cremation ghats, and to have one's ashes scattered into the holy Ganges river puts an immediate end to the cycles of birth and rebirth; thus, liberation.

*Bhagavad Gita:* lit., "Song of the Lord"; part of the epic Mahabharata, it contains a systematic statement of the perennial philosophy in the form of a dialogue between Krishna (the incarnation of the god Vishnu) and Arjuna, his chosen devotee.

*Bhagavan:* godhead; one who is full of light.

*bhakti:* ardent devotion and love of God.

*bhavana:* feeling, emotion, sensitivity; creative contemplation.

*bindu:* compact mass of Shakti gathered into an undifferentiated point ready to create.

*Brahma:* one god among many gods, Brahma is the creative spirit of the Hindu trinity, along with Vishnu (preserving, protecting) and Shiva* (dissolving, transforming). *However, in the form of Paramashiva, Shiva stands for the Absolute, God.

*Brahman:* the Absolute, pure foundational consciousness, the highest reality, the One.

*brahmachari:* one who practices brahmacharya.

*brahmacharya:* the first stage of life; a period of moral education during which celibacy is an important discipline.

*brahmaloka:* loka; region, place; one of the higher planes of existence; the world of Brahma.

*Brahmanadi:* the sushumna.

*Brahmarandhra:* the sahasrara chakra at the top of the head. See also chidakash/a.

*brahmin:* a member of the first of four orders of traditional Indian society. This order includes priests and intellectuals.

*buddhi:* (1) a category of the universe; (2) a faculty higher than manas (mind); it is the capacity or faculty of discrimination, ascertainment, decision, and will; intelligent will. In considering buddhi, chitta, and manas, it is important to note the difference between Eastern and Western interpretations of "mind." Eastern thinkers distinguish more finely between mental faculties. See chitta for a detailed discussion. In the Sutras, buddhi is used interchangeably with "subtle discrimination", "spiritual discernment", "the steady mind", "higher mind", "wisdom", and the like.

*chakra:* lit., wheel, circle; name given to the centers of conscious energy in the subtle body. Most scriptures cite seven of these centers, although in the Sutras, Nityananda alludes to a more numerous and complex system. The chakras are associated with the sushumna nadi and flanked on the left and right by the ida and pingala nadis. These nerves and centers are not biological. When the kundalini is awakened, it travels up the sushumna, passing through the chakras. Consciousness widens as each higher chakra is crossed, until the final goal is reached when the kundalini energy merges with its source, the energy of life itself, in the Brahmarandhra.

*chidakash/a: chit\*:* absolute consciousness, *akash/a:* subtle inner space; thus "sky of consciousness." In the Sutras, also synonymous with: sky of the heart, heart-sky, heart-space, akasha. See also: Brahmarandhra, sahasrara chakra, prana linga, Shiva linga, abode of Shiva, still point, thousand-petaled lotus, Brahmaloka. \*In Sanskrit, the root "chit" becomes "chid" when followed by "akasha."

*chit:* Absolute Consciousness.

*chitta:* individual consciousness, the mind of the empirical individual that is composed of three elements: *buddhi:* the ascertaining intelligence; it gives name and meaning to the perceptions of manas; *ahamkar:* the I-consciousness, the power of self-appropriation, ego; *manas:* the perceiving intelligence, with the senses, builds up perceptions and images, limited mind. In the Sutras, as in general English usage, "mind" is often used as a synonym for both "chitta" as well as the more limited "manas."

*dandi:* from "danda" meaning "staff"; thus, one who has a staff. A particular order of sannyasis, one of the ten orders of monks organized by Shankara, are known as the dandi swamis and are identified by the staff they carry.

*darshan:* lit., seeing; (1) the act of seeing the Divinity within the guru or within the representation of the Divine as in a sculpture or painting; (2) a system of philosophy.

*dharana:* lit., holding; holding an object in attention or consciousness, perfect concentration of the mind.

*dharma:* lit., that which holds; moral principle, "that which is decreed" by scripture as duty; Law.

*dhyana:* meditation; an unbroken flow of thought toward the object of concentration. This unbroken flow is the goal of the practice of dharana.

*Gita:* see Bhagavad Gita.

*Gopala:* the form of Krishna as cow-tender.

*Govinda:* lit., giver of enlightenment; a name of Krishna.

*Gujarat:* province on the northwest coast of India, north of Bombay.

*guna:* (1) the three primary constituent gunas of Prakriti are tamas (inertia), rajas (passion, activity), and sattva (balance, light, illumination); (2) quality, property, or attribute.

*guru:* a channel or medium of the grace-bestowing power of God, a perfected spiritual master who has realized identity with the Divine and who can impart this experience to a disciple; the teacher.

*Hara:* a god; one name of Shiva; means one who has conquered himself.

*Hari:* a god; one name of Vishnu or his incarnations (like Krishna); Hari literally means "one who steals," in this context, one who steals the hearts of the devotees.

*harijan: hari:* god, *jan:* people, so "people of god," the term was popularized by Gandhi in his attempt to improve the lot of the outcastes.

*hatha yoga:* method of obtaining salvation employing vital energy flowing through the nadis; in this yoga, great importance is given to physical fitness; supernormal powers are obtained as a result of the practice of this yoga.

*heart-space:* see hridayakasha

*hridaya:* lit., heart; the mystic center.

*hridayakasha: dridaya:* heart; akasha: space; translated as "sky of the heart," "heart-space," and the like. In the Sutras, synonymous with the Brahmarandhra, the place in the head where ida, pingala, and sushumna merge, where kundalini is one with the Atman.

*ida:* one of the three primary nadis or channels for the flow of life-energy; the ida begins on the left and with its counterpart, the pingala, criss-crosses over the central sushumna. All three join and culminate in the Brahmarandhra or the sahasrara chakra. See also nadi.

*japa:* devotional exercise consisting in the repetition of a mantra or the name of a deity.

*jiva:* see jivatman

*jivatman:* individual (Self incarnated in a body).

*jivanmukti: jivan:* while alive, mukti: liberation; liberation while alive.

*jnana:* spiritual wisdom.

*jnanamrita:* the nectar of spiritual wisdom.

*jnani:* lit., person of spiritual wisdom; one who has realized the Self.

*Kanakadasa:* a saint belonging to a low caste and refused admission to the Krishna temple in Udipi by the high-caste brahmins. He therefore went to the rear of the temple wall to peek through an aperture; the Krishna image turned 180 degrees to give him darshan. Even to this day, while the temple faces east (as temples normally do), the image faces west.

*karma:* (1) act, work, action; according to Hindu philosophical thought, every action performed with desire for its fruit produces an effect and leaves behind a residue which imprisons the soul in the world of existence; (2) law of causation governing action and its effects; moral law.

*Kashi:* see Benares

*kumbhak/a:* retention of the breath.

*kumkum:* vermilion powder used in rituals.

*kundalini:* lit., coiled up; the creative power of Shiva, that aspect of Shakti that lies coiled in three and a half folds in muladhara chakra at the base of the spine. This shakti can be awakened by a guru through the process of shaktipat. The main aim of spiritual practice is to rouse this power in man and pass it through the chakras in the sushumna nadi. The seventh chakra is the sahasrara; for the kundalini to reach this point is the highest goal.

*linga/m:* lit., a sign; (I) as the symbol of Shiva it is revered in the form of a stone post or egg in Shaivite temples or shrines; it is a symbol of Shiva's formless form; (2) the subtle space containing the whole universe in the process of formation and dissolution.

*maha:* great, high.

*Mahabharata:* ancient Hindu epic collection; contains eighteen books, including the Bhagavad Gita.

*mahatma/n:* great Self or great soul, realized soul.

*mahasamadhi:* lit., great resolution, great resolving; when speaking of a saint, it is the conscious shedding of the physical body.

*mahashanti:* the great peace; the highest peace, peace that passes all understanding.

*manas:* limited mind; that mental faculty which coordinates the work of the senses, bringing images and perceptions back to the subtle body (it is then the function of buddhi to discriminate among the images and ascertain their meaning). See also chitta.

*mantra:* sacred word or formula to be chanted; formulated to awaken the spiritual energy by constant repetition. A japa is normally given by a guru to the disciple to suit his predisposition.

*maya:* lit., that which measures; (1) the power that measures or limits; (2) the cosmic process or limiting force of the Infinite responsible for the sense of duality.

*mind:* in the Sutras, used both as a synonym for chitta, the entire, three-component mental apparatus, and as a synonym for manas, limited mind.

*moksha:* liberation

*mouna:* silence; vow of silence.

*mukti:* liberation.

*muladhara:* chakra located at the base of the spine.

*nadi:* the channels through which conscious creative energy and prana (vital breath) circulate in the subtle body.

*nidra:* sleep, as in: tamo-nidra (gross sleep) or yoga-nidra (subtle state).

*nijananda: nija:* one's own, *ananda:* bliss; bliss of one's own Self.

*nirguna: nir:* without, *guna:* quality; without quality, feature, or attribute.

*nirvikalpa:* a state of consciousness free of all thought-constructs.

*nityananda:* eternal bliss.

*Om:* sacred syllable that is Brahman itself as sound; the ultimate, primeval sound.

*Omkar: kar:* from the root *kri,* to do; thus the sound or power of Om.

*para:* the highest; the Absolute (usually seen as a prefix).

*parabrahma:* the Absolute; God.

*paramahamsa:* lit., supreme swan; the mythical swan Hamsa is reputed to have been capable of drawing milk out of a mixture of milk and water. A paramahamsa is therefore a realized person who can distinguish real from unreal.

*paramananda:* bliss of the highest, bliss of the Absolute.

*Paramatman:* lit., Supreme Self, synonymous with Atman.

*Parvati:* goddess; consort of Shiva (Shiva here referring to one god of the Hindu trinity).

*pingala:* one of the three principal nadis.

*Prakriti:* unconscious cosmic Nature; the energy that evolves as the world.

*prana:* (1) that force which animates, vital force, vital air, the universal life-force; (2) in the human organism, prana has five functions, the first of which, the out-breath, is also called prana. Prana as life-force is the natural connecting link between consciousness and its physical manifestations.

*prana linga:* the spiritual form of Shiva the Absolute.

*pranava:* resonance; used to designate the syllable Om; the universal sound.

*prana-shakti:* the divine Shakti working both in the universe and in the individual (in the individual, kundalini is the form or expression of this Shakti).

*prana vayu:* the breath of life; vital force, the life-force or energy.

*prema:* devotional love.

*puja:* worship or ritual.

*puraka:* the inhaled breath.

*Puranas:* lit., ancient; a collection of symbolical and allegorical writings, mythological in character; there are eighteen such scriptures.

*puri:* lit., abode; hence, as suffix denotes city or village, as in Ganeshpuri; "abode or village of Ganesha."

*purna:* perfect; full of divine consciousness.

*Purusha:* (1) the Self, pure conscious being; (2) in Sankya philosophy, Spirit in contradistinction to Prakriti, cosmic Nature (unconscious energy from which the world evolves); (3) in literary Sanskrit, commonly rendered "man."

*raja yoga:* lit., the king of yogas; emphasized mental and spiritual discipline rather than physical culture. In the Sutras, Nityananda uses raja yoga to denote the highest yoga; that which is non-dual and indivisible—the continuous, unbroken awareness of the Self.

*rajas:* one of the three primary gunas; the principle of motion, activity, passion, and pain.

**Ramayana:** great epic of Hindu literature; along with the Puranas and the later epic Mahabharata, it forms the foundation of Indian historical writing. It tells the story of Rama and Sita; according to the scriptures, Rama is the seventh incarnation of Vishnu, and Sita is his divine consort. The Ramayana tells of the abduction of Sita by the ten-headed Ravana, a powerful evil king of Sri Lanka, and her subsequent rescue. In the fight with Ravana, Rama is helped by Hanuman (subsequently venerated as a great devotee) and by Rama's brother Lakshmana.

*rechaka:* the exhaled breath.

**Rig Veda:** first and most ancient of four Vedas, perhaps dating from as early as 1000 BC (dates disputed).

*rishi:* lit., seer; wise man or sage; the hymns of the Vedas are said to have been revealed to the rishis of ancient India.

*sadhana:* pursuit of an ideal; the practice of spiritual discipline.

*sadhu:* lit., good, holy; a holy man.

*sahasrar/a:* lit., thousand; highest chakra of the subtle body, symbolized by a thousand-petaled lotus or a thousand-spoked wheel; where kundalini unites with Shiva; seat of pure consciousness.

*samadhi:* lit., resolution, resolving, "drawing together of the mind"; extraordinary state in which the fluctuations of the mind are stilled; superconscious state. There are two types of samadhi: *sa-vikalpa* in which distinction between subject and object is retained, and *nir-vikalpa* in which the yogi realizes his total one-ness (union) with the Absolute.

*samsara:* lit., movement; existence in the phenomenal world of contradictions and dualities.

*sannyasa:* renunciation.

*sannyasi:* lit., one who casts away, renounces; one who has renounced worldly bonds in order to devote him/herself to the spiritual life.

*sat-chit-ananda:* being-consciousness-bliss; the three-fold description of Brahman, the Absolute: *sat*: the essence of existence, "be-ness"; *chit*: consciousness; and *ananda*: bliss, joy, ecstasy.

*sattva:* one of the three primary gunas; the principle of being, light, happiness, and harmony; essence; balance.

*Self:* self-existence, pure awareness and pure consciousness, self-luminous, and according to some schools of philosophy, also self-conscious; only one Self is manifested in all minds and bodies.

*shabda:* sound.

*Shakti:* power; active, creative power of the Divine.

*shanti:* peace.

*Shiva:* (1) the Absolute; pure consciousness, the transcendent divine principle; (2) one of the gods of the Hindu trinity, along with Vishnu and Brahma.

*shraddha:* intense faith, deeper than mind; involves both knowledge and will or dynamism; it is also held to indicate a pleasant inclination toward yoga.

*shuddha bhavana: shuddha:* pure; *bhavana:* feeling, thought, contemplation.

*shudra:* one belonging to the fourth order of traditional Indian society.

*siddhi:* lit., accomplishment, achievement; power attained through yogic practice.

*shunya:* (Buddhism): the void, emptiness; state in which no object is experienced.

*sushumna:* one of the primary nadis; the middle or central channel for the flow of the life-energy.

*sushupti:* state of deep, dreamless sleep; one of man's four states of consciousness: *jagrat*: waking, *svapna*: dreaming, *sushupti*: deep sleep, and *turiya*: the fourth, the Atman.

*swami:* lit., master of one's Self; title given to monks and religious heads of maths (temples).

*swarajya:* lit., kingdom of the Self, hence an attribute of Atman implying perfect freedom. In the political sense it means freedom from foreign rule, and so self-government.


*tamo-nidra:* state of gross sleep.

*tamas:* one of the three primary gunas; principle of quality of inertia, insensitivity, and delusion.

*tapas:* lit., heat.

*tapasya:* lit., that which generates heat or energy; brooding, incubation; the concentration of energy to generate creative force.

*tattva:* "thatness," the very being of a thing; principle or category.

*turiya:* lit., the fourth; the fourth state of consciousness beyond the states of waking, dreaming, and deep sleep and stringing together all the states; the transcendental Self.

*upadhi:* limiting adjunct or condition; obstacle.

*upanayana:* initiation ceremony undergone by all young high-caste Hindu males at about the age of seven before going to the guru for education.

*vairagya:* (1) intense dispassion for worldliness, not colored by desire; (2) desirelessness; (3) renunciation.

*vasana:* lit., smell; impregnation, residual trace left by any act; tendency, habit energy; generally applied to indicate tendency, predisposition or latency at birth as a result of character and action in previous incarnations.

*vayu:* (1) air, the fourth element; (2) the vital air, vital force, the breath of life, the life-force: prana.

*Veda:* from the root "vid" meaning "to know," "veda" literally means "wisdom." the Vedas, edited by the great Vyasa, constitute the knowledge of God revealed to seers at the beginning of each cycle. There are four Vedas: Rig, Yajur, Sama, and Atharva. Each is divided into four parts: Samhita (hymns), Brahmana (rituals), Aranyaka (to be read in retirement in the forest after one's fulfillment of worldly responsibilities—aranya is forest) and Upanishad (lit., "sit near;" that is, sit near the guru).

*Vedanta:* lit., the end or goal of the Vedas (anta : end); a system of philosophy based on the Vedas. Nityananda uses both of these terms, Veda and Vedanta, to indicate philosophical scholarship in general.

*vibhuti:* (1) lit., force of God used to manifest extraordinary people or things in which this force manifests; (2) any object so manifested; (3) ash (by derivation, since ash has often been the object miraculously manifested).

*vishva-prana:* lit., universal energy.

*yajna:* Vedic ritual; sacrifice or fire ceremony.

*yantra:* symbolic drawing or visual contemplative device; the yantra represents the cosmos and is often used as an aid to concentration.

*yoga:* In the Sutras, the science through which individuals recognize their essential identity with God; awareness, transformation of human consciousness into divine consciousness.

*yoga-nidra:* subtle sleep, sleep of awareness.

*yogi:* lit., united; one who studies and practices yoga, who is absorbed in spiritual practices with the sole intent of uniting the individual with the universal.

*yukti:* reason, argument, cleverness, skill.

# About Captain M.U. Hatengdi

M.U. Hatengdi was born in 1914 in Mangalore, India. His early education was in the local G.H. School and Government College. In 1936 he obtained his Honours/ Masters degree in Economics from Presidency College, Madras. From 1941 through 1964, Captain Hatengdi made his career in the Indian Navy and retired as Naval Secretary at Naval Headquarters, New Delhi. He was immediately appointed Commercial Manager in the government-owned Mazagaon Dock. Soon after, he was made the General Manager and Chairman of the Board of Administration of the Canteen Stores Department. His second retirement came in 1970, and he has since involved himself in activities connected with social organizations and religious trust.

Captain Hatengdi received his first darshan of Bhagavan Nityananda in 1943 and remained a loving devotee throughout the years. He has served as Chairman of the Sri

Nityananda Arogyashram Trust, which established and maintains a charitable hospital in Ganeshpuri. He is the author of *Nityananda: The Divine Presence* (Rudra Press, 1984), a book of stories and reminiscences about the life of Nityananda.

# About Swami Chetanananda

American-born Swami Chetanananda brings a contemporary Western perspective to his articulation of the wisdom of Nityananda. Chetanananda was initiated into the ancient Saraswati order of monks in 1978 in Ganeshpuri, India. In 1981, he founded the Nityananda Institute, now headquartered in Portland, Oregon. He also directs the Rudrananda Ashram, a Portland-based community of people living a practical spiritual life. Its teaching and meditation practice are derived from the ancient Kashmir Shaivite traditions. The Ashram is named for Swami Rudrananda (Rudi), an American spiritual teacher who was deeply influenced by his contacts with Nityananda. Swami Chetanananda assumed leadership of the Ashram on Rudi's passing in 1973. The Nityananda Institute is a not-for-profit center for meditation and quality living committed to making a spiritual life both understandable and accessible to Americans. It is named in loving gratitude for Nityananda of Ganeshpuri.

Swami Chetanananda is the author of numerous books and audiotapes on spiritual practice including *The Breath of God, The Open Moment, Will I Be the Hero of My Own Life,* and *Meditation: A Guided Practice for Every Day,* all published by Rudra Press.

# About Rudra Press

We hope you enjoy *The Sky of the Heart*. Rudra Press publishes the finest books, audios, and videos on spirituality, meditation, hatha yoga, health, and healing. Practical and powerful in their simple everyday approach, our products are designed to meet the needs of modern life. We support you in your quest for personal growth and transformation. Increased health, inner balance, and well-being are just a few of the many benefits that you may experience through your contact with our products.

## *Nityananda: The Divine Presence*
M.U. Hatengdi

Fascinating eyewitness stories and rare photographs trace Nityananda's life from the turn of the century to his passing in 1961. Considered one of the greatest saints of this century, Nityananda lived a life of austerity and simplicity.

His understanding and vision allowed miracles to sponta-
neously occur around him. Nityananda deeply touched
hundreds of thousands of lives. This book shares vivid stories of the power and love that surrounds one who is completely immersed in the Divine.

$14.95 • paperback • 177 pages • 0-915801-00-0

## *Will I Be the Hero of My Own Life?*

Swami Chetanananda

This book examines the criteria for becoming a hero and
delves into the question central to the heart of living life in
the spirit of inspiration. Drawing on historical examples
from the epic *Bhagavad Gita*, mystical poetry, and art, the
author explores the most difficult and challenging issues a
person encounters when undertaking an authentic spiritual
discipline. Although this journey may take you into the
darkest places in your mind and force you to confront your
deepest fears, it also promises the possibility of profound
freedom and a life lived in the spirit of creativity, integra-
tion, and happiness.

$14.95 • paperback • 200 pages • 0-915801-38-8

## The Open Moment
*Reflections on the Spiritual Life*

Swami Chetanananda

This beautiful collection of quotations addresses the essential points of leading a spiritual life and offers compelling perspective on gaining mastery over the mind, emotions, and desires. Rich, inspirational, and thought-provoking, these eloquent quotes direct the reader to an experience of the extraordinary power within—a subtle flow of energy that has historically been referred to as love, god, vital force, and other words used to communicate about the divine. Written with a non-denominational voice, this soothing book offers inspiration, upliftment, guidance, and wisdom.

$16.00 • Cloth • 120 pages • 0-915801-52-3

## The Breath of God
Swami Chetanananda

A compelling collection of essays which penetrate to the core of a spiritual quest. Based on twenty years of intense study and teaching, Swami Chetanananda offers refreshing answers to the questions and challenges one faces when embarking on a spiritual path. These essays are practical and inspiring—addressing stages in practice, mental discipline, dealing with fear and pain, and commitment to spiritual growth.

$15.95 • paperback • 310 pages • 0-915801-05-1

## Meditation
*A Guided Practice for Every Day*

Swami Chetanananda

This exceptional program guides the listener to an experience of meditation and stillness. Designed as an aid to daily meditation practice, Side A leads the listener through a powerful experience of meditation. Side B contains a discussion on the purpose and benefits of mediation and also an inspirational talk on what may be the most important choice a person has: the choice to be happy. Packaged with an 18-page booklet that introduces the fundamental principles for establishing your meditation practice. Formerly released as *Meditation: An Invitation to Growth*.

$12.95 • 90 minute audio tape and booklet • 0-915801-57-4

## The Logic of Love
Swami Chetanananda

Powerful essays discuss a constellation of themes about the logic of the heart, exploring what it means to let go—to surrender—and love. The author describes the logic established in the experience of love where one operates free of desire, selfish motive, and tension. Most people strive to live from a state of love, but they do not know how. This book provides the concrete techniques for living from a position of real strength.

$14.95 • paperback • 208 pages • 0-915801-34-5


## Keys to Mastery
Swami Chetanananda

In these audio tapes, the author describes the five essential steps to self-mastery and inner peace: instruction, practice, mental discipline, extending to others, and letting go.

$19.95 • 3-tape audio set • 210 minutes • 0-915801-23-X

## Entering Infinity
Swami Rudrananda (Rudi)

In this book, Rudi speaks about spiritual growth. For Rudi, the foundation of spiritual work centers on the wish to grow. As this wish matures in the process of spiritual development, it evolves into a deep love of God and a love of life. From this state of love, one is able to practice the ultimate act of love—one of surrender.

$16.95 • paperback • 210 pages • 0-915801-41-8

$10.95 • companion audio tape • 60 minutes • 0-915801-45-0


## Rudi in His Own Words
Swami Rudrananda

This book provides a window into the subtle spiritual state that Rudi attained. Here, Rudi speaks about transforming the energy in the tensions and stresses of your life into spiritual growth. The author describes how to practice this transformation on a daily basis—even as you talk to your boss, ride the subway, or reach out for love.

$14.95 • paperback • 197 pages • 0-915801-20-5

*Spiritual Cannibalism*
Swami Rudrananda

The author outlines the concepts of spiritual work and describes his life of disciplined practice and teaching. Rudi explores the basic human need to grow and describes a series of techniques fundamental to his spiritual understanding.

$14.95 • paperback • 182 pages • 0-915801-07-8

For more information on Rudra Press's complete line of products or to request a free catalog, please call or write:

RUDRA PRESS
PO Box 13390
Portland, OR 97213
tel. 1-800-876-7798
fax 1-503-235-0909